The Winds of Wisdom

Visions from the Thirty Enochian Aethyrs

The Winds of Wisdom

Visions from the Thirty Enochian Aethyrs

David Shoemaker

Originally published in 2016 by Nephilim Press

This paperback edition published in 2017 by

Anima Solis Books
P.O. Box 215483
Sacramento, California 95821, USA

livingthelema.com

Cover design by Frater Julianus

ISBN: 0-9893844-4-6
ISBN-13: 978-0-9893844-4-5

A∴A∴
Publication in Class B

Imprimatur:

N. Fra. A∴A∴		**PRO COLL. SUMM.**
I.	$7^\circ=4^\square$	**PRO COLL. INT.**
V.V.	$6^\circ=5^\square$	
I.	Praem.	**PRO COLL. EXT.**
R.O.	Imp.	
L.L.L.	Canc.	

OTHER WORKS BY DAVID SHOEMAKER

As Author

Living Thelema: A Practical Guide to Attainment in Aleister Crowley's System of Magick

Various essays, published in the journals *Mezlim, Agape, Black Pearl, Neshamah, and Cheth*

Living Thelema (podcast)

As Editor

Karl Germer: Selected Letters 1928-1962

Phyllis Seckler (Soror Meral): The Thoth Tarot, Astrology, & Other Selected Writings

Phyllis Seckler (Soror Meral): Kabbalah, Magick, & Thelema. Selected Writings Vol. II

Jane Wolfe: The Cefalu Diaries 1920-1923

As Musician and Composer

Elsa Letterseed Original Score

Workings (2000-2010)

Last Three Lives (self-titled)

Last Three Lives: Via

TABLE OF CONTENTS

ACKNOWLEDGEMENTS

My deepest gratitude goes to Frater Julianus for his beautiful cover design, and to Lauren Gardner and Amy Bauer for proofreading and editorial suggestions.

And as always, all my love to my family, to my students and colleagues, and to my wonderful partner Liz.

NOTE ON THE USE OF GENDER-SPECIFIC PRONOUNS

Throughout this book, I have attempted to use gender-neutral wording, or to alternate the use of masculine and feminine pronouns when giving generic examples of ritual actions, initiatory processes, and the like. The visions themselves, including the outline of the ritual incorporating eroto-comotose lucidity used to obtain the vision of the 8th Aethyr, are consistently worded in masculine terms, inasmuch as these are my personal diary entries and workings.

INTRODUCTION

In the mysteries of your creation, in faith, she lives,
In the shrine of the winds of Wisdom.

—The angel AZIZ,
from the vision of the 27th Aethyr

Do what thou wilt shall be the whole of the Law.

Magicians are explorers.

We delve into the depths of our own unconscious minds. We experiment with techniques drawn from a diversity of ages and cultures around the world. We venture into regions of the so-called astral world in search of deeper truths about ourselves and our universe.

As any earthly explorer will tell you, a well-drawn map is your best friend. Just so, those of us setting out to explore the spiritual worlds need a good map to guide us—or at least to aid us as we try to organize and make sense of our experiences. The system of Enochian magick developed by John Dee and Edward Kelley in the 16th century is one such magical map, and their approach to exploring (*scrying*) the so-called 30 Aethyrs is the central focus of this book. These Aethyrs are conceived as layers of astral real estate, with each successive layer (from the 30th moving to the 1st) representing ever more exalted and ineffable states of consciousness, ruled by so-called "Governors". Accordingly, the further one attempts to venture into these realms, the more personal and spiritual development is required to get useful results.

The names, structure, and basic nature of these Aethyrs were discovered and developed gradually by Dee and Kelly over the course of several years, but we could hardly say that they made the most of their discoveries during their lifetimes. That task has fallen to modern magicians, including the various Adepts of the Hermetic

Order of the Golden Dawn, and of course Aleister Crowley. Crowley's experiments with scrying the 30 Aethyrs were recorded in his monumental work, *The Vision and the Voice,* and many modern magicians have followed in his footsteps, attempting to explore these regions for themselves.

It is not the purpose of this present book to give a comprehensive overview of the system of the 30 Aethyrs, or to be a full-scale practical manual. Readers interested in this sort of material can do no better than to seek out my friend Lon Milo DuQuette's excellent *Enochian Vision Magick.* Rather, my purpose here is to present my own scrying results, obtained over the course of several years of work, in service to the ideals of Scientific Illuminism; that is, to leave a detailed record of my explorations, so that others might benefit from my little additions to the cosmic map.

In undertaking these visions, I adopted an experimental "hypothesis" that the Aethyrs might be mapped out across the various *sephiroth* (spheres) of the Qabalistic Tree of Life. Specifically, I conceived of Aethyrs 1-10 as corresponding to the ten sephiroth in the Qabalistic "world" of Atziluth; Aethyrs 11-20 in Briah; and finally, Aethyrs 21-30 in the world of Yetzirah. My experiences convinced me that this is a potent and workable scheme, but as they say, your mileage may vary. Additional avenues of exploration included taking note of potential correspondences to Sun and Moon placement at the time of the working, the Yetziratic (e.g. elemental, zodiacal, Tarot) attributions of the Name of the Aethyr being explored, and the Enochian elemental Tablet (or Tablets) on which the Governors' names appear. Looking back at the results, I have concluded that Sun and Moon placement (I used the tropical zodiac in this record) may have some influence over the character of the vision and the guides that come forth. The influence of the Elemental tablets was less apparent, but the Yetziratic attributions of the Aethyr names were clearly central to the visions.

I should comment on my relationship to the Enochian language itself throughout these visions. While I had worked extensively with the Enochian system prior to these visions, I had not studied the language itself in any depth. Accordingly, when I "heard" and subsequently spoke the Enochian passages in the visions, I had no conscious knowledge of their meaning. Furthermore, I did not attempt to translate them until all the visions were complete. This is, to me, a striking validation of the power and utility of the Enochian system.

Many practitioners of Enochian magick (including Crowley himself) have noted that the magician's own personal and spiritual growth is necessary in between many visions. She must integrate the experiences and instructions obtained in one vision before moving on to the next. Sometimes this may be as simple as nodding one's head inwardly at the truth revealed in a vision, and moving on to the next Aethyr the very next day. At other times, it may require many months of careful analysis and meditation, or even sweeping changes in one's external life, to fully integrate the vision and move on. As Crowley noted in reference to his own exploration of the Aethyrs, in *Magick in Theory and Practice*, Cap. XVIII:

> The Adept who explored these Aethyrs did not have to pass through and beyond the Universe, the whole of which yet lies within even the inmost (30th) Aethyr. He was able to summon the Aethyrs he wanted, and His chief difficulty was that sometimes He was at first unable to pierce their veils. In fact, as the Book shows, it was only by virtue of successive and most exalted initiations undergone in the Aethyrs themselves that He was able to penetrate beyond the 15th. The Guardians of such fortresses know how to guard.

My own experience with these visions definitely bore this out. The early visions tended to be brief and (at least compared to many of the later ones) less remarkable. Their content was often more general in character, with much less of the distinctly personal material that came through in later visions. It was almost as if, in these early visions, I was retreading territory already explored, and I had to penetrate further into the Aethyrs before the truly distinctive material would come forth full-force. Perhaps unsurprisingly, my progress matched up with formal initiatory steps I had, or had not, completed at the time of the vision. At various points I had to make major changes in my inner and outer world before proceeding. Sometimes I realized this fact right away and set to work. At other times I would simply find myself unable, unwilling, or unmotivated to proceed, only discovering the reasons why months later when I found myself suddenly empowered to move ahead, and reflected on my own transformation during the intervening time.

With all that said, I'm not making any grand claims of personal attainment based on this material. I am simply presenting it as it stands, for its potential value as a record of my work, in keeping with the spirit of Scientific Illuminism. My hope is that it will be useful and inspiring to those of you who might wish to undertake these explorations in service of your own growth and transformation. I have included relevant resources and a suggested working methodology in Part Two of this book, to make it easier for you to try these experiments on your own.

These visions were, and still are, incredibly moving, meaningful and transformative for me, and many of the discoveries and insights contained in them have found their way into the systems of initiation I administer. I certainly hope you will find them inspiring and stimulating, but they may not mean much to you or anyone else. As always, *your own* experimentation will bring you to those Truths which are most necessary for your progress, and may Light, Life, Love and Liberty be with you in your journey.

Love is the law, love under will.

Sacramento, California
April 10, 2016 e.v.
Anno Legis V^{ii}

Part One:

The Visions

THE CRY OF THE 30TH AETHYR, WHICH IS CALLED TEX[1]

First Vision

Monday, September 17, 2007. Approximately 2pm. Sol in Virgo, Luna in Sagittarius.

I rise to a moonlit landscape, with great mountains in the distance. The terrain is desert-like. The moon is three-quarters full.

A Hermit bearing a lantern and staff appears before me and approaches, just to the left and in front of me. I test him and he passes.

He beckons me with his staff to walk forward into the plain in front of me. A stairway leading downward into the earth appears before me.

There is a great gem, perfectly cut and diamond-like in appearance. It is warmly lit here, like a little workshop. Letters in English appear below the gem: ZAZ.[2] I ask for more information. He says this is his name. I ask for instruction, and he speaks:

Go to the heights, not the depths.
The Stone[3] is on high as it is here.

---

[1] Leo, Virgo, Spirit. Malkuth in Yetzirah. Governors' names appear on the Tablet of Water.

[2] Zayin, Aleph, Zayin=15=זח, "he who impels".

[3] A foreshadowing of the Seer's vision of the 5th Aethyr, LIT. Also, this entire passage recalls the traditional doctrine, "Kether is in Malkuth."

The Peak of Light.
I ask for further instruction, and he continues:

This is the world beyond the World.
The Earth that changes.
Here sometimes, and sometimes Not,
For it is in another Form.

I thank ZAZ and return up the stairs, and the Vision is ended.

Second Vision

Monday, September 24, 2007. Approximately 11pm. Sol in Libra, Luna in Pisces.

I rise to a great height. I arrive at the same landscape as in the previous vision. There is lightning in the sky and the mountains are once again visible in the distance. The stairs and the pit are before me. ZAZ approaches me across the desert. A creature also appears to my right, first appearing as a goat, low to the ground. Its features are indistinct, and it walks slowly toward me.

I vibrate TEX again, and whole scene is now swirling…a swirling vortex. I am taken into the center…ah, the garden, deep and lush green. Green leaves, and a maiden. She is fair-skinned, with blonde hair, and she wears a white dress. I test her and she fails. I move onward and inward.

I am with ZAZ again. I now behold his face…a bearded, aged male with a ruddy complexion. Not decrepit, just somewhat aged, around the mid-50s. He bears a staff in his left hand, gesturing toward the mountains.

It is twilight. We walk together toward the mountains, across a plain. The earth is dry and cracked, with shrubs like weeds. I don't see a moon at first, and then I do…it is now waxing and near full, almost directly above me and just slightly to the right.

There is an opening to a cave in the side of a mountain. I am instructed to go into the cave and place my hands on the cubical stone at the center and back of the cave. A light pours in from an opening directly above it.

There is a circular disc, concave, lined with lapis, like a bowl reflecting the canopy of heaven. It is empty but for the reflection of the golden stars in the lapis itself.

I am to make my mind as this bowl—a reflection of the celestial cosmos—yet firmly supported by the material. This is the Yetziratic component of Earth, behind and above the physical.

I ask for more instruction. Water is poured into the bowl, and my mind feels full. I shrink to a very small size, swimming in the bowl. I realize the task is to emerge from it—not succumb to it—so that I may bear the bowl. I must make my mind as the reflection of the canopy of heaven as in the bowl, rather than drown in it.

I ask for more instruction—there is none tonight—and the Vision is ended.

THE CRY OF THE 29TH AETHYR, WHICH IS CALLED RII[4]

Tuesday, September 25, 2007. About 9.30 pm. Sol in Libra, Luna in Pisces.

[Diary note: I went to the temple for preparatory banishings and the Star Sapphire: I experienced an incredibly strong current and reflux at the receptive climax of the Star Sapphire—torrential, spasmodic, full-body shuddering. Completely full of the light. A Vision during the signs of NOX: the milk of the stars flowing forth from me as the Mother. The Seed flowing forth into the mother as the Father, the Word. The Father and the Mother together giving birth to the Child and the World. The Diamond Body as Kether, Chokmah, Binah and Tiphareth.]

The Vision of RII begins:

Rising to a great height. I am underwater yet there is lightning. And many fish, large and small. More lightning, repeated and powerful.

I am approached by a humanoid, fish-headed being. He is thrice tested and thrice passed. He gives his name as Mophas. I ask for spelling in a language intelligible to me, and he gives Maim, Vav, Peh, Aleph, Samekh.[5]

---

[4] Pisces, Sagittarius, Sagittarius. Yesod in Yetzirah. Governors' names appear on the Tablet of Earth.

[5] מֻופאס=187=זקף, "lifted up".

I ask for instruction. We move quickly through the water, swimming, as lightning continues to strike through the water, all around us. There is an underwater volcano, and we enter it. I am surrounded by FIRE! I am of the fire, projected upward as in the blazing arrow of the path of Sagittarius. A voice cries:

Blast thou forth from the underworld!
The undercurrents of Fire send forth thy soul unto the heights!
The flame is constant, the rise eternal.
The aspiration…that arrow…ever burning, ever flying,
An endless, undying, serpentine, splendorous movement of Fire!
All things aspiring unto the light from their station unto the next.
The Secret Fire forcing upward, ever forcing upward.[6]

I weaken, and will myself to return to my body after thanking Mophas. May the blessings of all the Aethyr RII be upon thee!

The Vision is ended.

---

[6] These images and phrases are all suggestive of Yesod, and of subconsciousness generally: An underworld, mostly unknown to the conscious mind, that nurtures the Secret Fire—the Life-Power or kundalini. Note also the correspondence of Sagittarius imagery to the path of Samekh, which emerges from Yesod to connect with Tiphareth.

THE CRY OF THE 28TH AETHYR, WHICH IS CALLED BAG[7]

Wednesday, September 26, 2007. 11pm. Sol in Libra, Luna in Aries.

Banishing by Fiat. A deep communion with ∑.[8] The Vision begins:

Rising…very rapidly. I behold an orange sky, and a vast desert dotted with pyramids.[9] There is a ram-headed statue in front of the nearest pyramid.

A bull-headed humanoid in Egyptian garb approaches, dark-skinned and muscular. I test him and he passes. He gives his name as Zizys. Zayin, Yod, Zayin, Yod, Samekh.[10]

I ask for instruction. The ram statue moves to the side, and an opening appears in the pyramid, revealing steps leading slightly downward. I enter, and soon find myself in the center of the pyramid. The ceiling is about 20 feet above me, with the center open to the sky. The pyramid is golden on the exterior and a

---

7 Aries, Taurus, Cancer. Hod in Yetzirah. Governors' names appear on the Tablet of Earth.

8 S is the first letter of the Name of the Seer's Holy Guardian Angel. ∑ is used to signify the Angel's Name throughout this work.

9 Symbols of Hod/Mercury

10 גיחזיון=94, "the valley of vision". This is also the total numeration of the "four powers and the seven delights and the twelve emancipations, and the two and twenty Privileges and the nine and forty Manifestations" referenced in Crowley's Vision of the 14th Aethyr. Thus, perhaps, is Zizys a herald of the Visions yet to come.

reddish brown on the inside. I behold a large statue of a lion, which is magically aflame. Zizys has come in behind me.

There seem to be passages directly across from me, opposite the entry door, leading out on the far side. I ask again for instruction, and a mighty voice responds:

Go not into the infernal realm, the flame shall carry thee up.
Go not into the darkness—the light shall lead thee forth.
Follow the fire; ever the fire.
For flame consumes the dross.
Sit before the feet of thy Angel.
Cry out in longing, in pain, and in joy.
Shatter the pyramid with thy ecstasy,
Then shall the true Light descend upon thee.

What is thy name? It is Glory.[11]
Thy true name, hidden from the sins of ages.
Thy pastors are sheep; the old aeon is done.
It hath spit thee out—yea, the universe hath spit thee out,
Like a seed from a fruit.
But the seed is planted, the tree shall grow,
And the fruit shall nourish.

I grow weary, and I am told there is to be no more instruction at this time. I am led out of the pyramid; the ram statue moves to close the entrance behind me. Zizys bows, and I give him blessing and thanks in the name of BAG. The scene swirls, becoming a vortex, and I am drawn in. I find myself speeding back to earth. I see my body, and the Vision is ended.

---

[11] A name of Hod

ZAA

THE CRY OF THE 27TH AETHYR, WHICH IS CALLED ZAA[12]

Tuesday, October 2, 2007. 11:15pm. Sol in Libra, Luna in Cancer.

Rising quickly, very quickly, to a great height. Stars, stars, galaxies…whirling about me.

A great giant appears, bearded and crowned. He is garbed in a green cloak, with a blue undergarment visible in places, and he wears a sunburst pendant upon his chest. He has crushed the universe, and all the galaxies are spinning away. All in an orb, a great spherical mass of All.

A great cross appears in the sky with a circle at the center, and I enter into it. I am taken in at great speed. Ahh…the circle-center of the cross is the yoni, and the folds of Her who is Naught. The great circle is the yoni, the Naught is the yoni. The All-Father has sent me into the center of the Cross.[13] A voice booms in Enochian:

Aziz[14] zir. A Zip par glo miam.
Tol vaoan zonac orocha.
A gono fifis piap.
A talho znurza canilu arphe.
Odo cicle qaa od zamran a babalond.
A cicle qaa a gono apila pii,

---

[12] Leo, Taurus, Taurus. Netzach of Yetzirah. Governors' names appear on the Tablet of Earth.

[13] These symbols suggest the devotional and tantric aspects of Netzach, as well as higher mysteries.

[14] A Kerubic angel and companion of Ziza. Fire of Fire.

A loholo ozongon ananael.[15]

Thus spake the space…the space within…the enwombed Adept in the yoni. The great glowing purple-pink voluptuous softness of All.

The sky above opens—vast and green, and a green field appears beneath it—all around me. The night sky above yet it is daytime. There is light, there is sky. The wind blows through fields of tall grass – enormous blades of green grass.

The Amazon[16] is here. She gently grazes the grass with her hand, glancing at me with one voluptuous eye…seductive and beckoning.

I see a moon and a sun in the sky. They fuse together into one sigil. Ahh… white brilliance extinguishes all but Itself.

And I have returned.

---

[15]Roughly:

Aziz I am. In ZIP all things have their continuance.
All truth is clothed therein.
In faith, carry out the balancing.
Into the Cup of thy Oath the blood will descend.
Open the mysteries of your creation and appear as a whore.
In the mysteries of your creation, in faith, she lives,
In the shrine of the winds of Wisdom.

This is a foreshadowing of the Seer's vision of the 9th Aethyr (ZIP). It is important to note that at the time of the scrying of the 27th Aethyr, the Seer had not studied the Enochian language intensively, although he was well acquainted with the alphabet, and had worked extensively with the Tablets. The close correspondence of the present Vision with the eventual Vision of the 9th Aethyr (which occurred more than two years later) is a compelling piece of evidence for the system's authenticity, especially since the Seer had made no effort to translate these Enochian lines in the intervening time.

[16] The "Magical Image" of Netzach

THE CRY OF THE 26TH AETHYR, WHICH IS CALLED DES[17]

Wednesday, October 3, 2007. 9:15 pm. Sol in Libra, Luna in Virgo.

I have risen to a brightly sunlit land, on the peak of a hill, overlooking a lush valley. Small homes dot the landscape, a beautiful, rural setting. The sun is large overhead, and beneath it is a crescent moon, with points upward. Yods rain down upon me from the Sun. The sunlight itself is composed of Yods.

A Hermit appears, an aged man wearing a brown cloak, and he holds his lantern aloft. Twin pillars[18] appear, as stone statues—soldiers, it seems--one to my left, the other to my right. I stand centered between them, and they also frame the sun and the moon in the sky.

The Hermit stands to my left. Within the Hermit's lantern the flame is the sun itself, yet tiny, the seed of the sun. Before me is a door, and he bids me enter.

It is blackness. It is blackness.

Another sun appears here, this one sickly, amidst the darkness. Blue green tears of sunlight fall upon me.[19] As I vibrate DES once more, I am removed from this sad chamber.

---

17 Spirit, Virgo, Gemini. Tiphareth in Yetzirah. Governors' names appear on the Tablet of Earth.

18 The Twins of Gemini

19 The tone and appearance of this section suggests the Qlippoth of Virgo.

I move back out into the sunlight under the full sky. The Yods rain down on me once more, and are absorbed into me. I am become liquid sunlight. A voice says:

Const vorz ji.
A DES sald a Mad par.
Same toh farzm od gono ovof.[20]

The sky is rent asunder. The statues come alive and march inward, crushing together in a cataclysm.

Turning to dust, the sky folds in on itself. The whole landscape becomes as small as a pinpoint before me. I reach out my palms, upturned and together, and the pinpoint of this universe falls into them. This in turn becomes a tunnel, white light streaking all around.

Faster and faster, I am drawn into the tunnel. A voice says:

Zar a Mad piaf.[21]

And it is all white brilliance...white brilliance. Now yellow-gold. Now rose-pink. Now black. Now black-rayed gold.[22] And I find I have returned.

---

20 Roughly:

Thunder is over you.
In DES is the wonder of God in them.
Know that the triumph is lifted up, and faith is magnified.

21 Roughly: The Course of God is in Balance.

22 These are, respectively, Queen Scale Kether, Queen Scale Tiphareth, King Scale Tiphareth, Queen Scale Malkuth (partial), and Princess Scale Malkuth, roughly tracing the descent of the Seer's consciousness back to his physical body.

THE CALL OF THE 25TH AETHYR, WHICH IS CALLED VTI[23]

Wednesday, October 24, 2007. Approximately 7:30pm. Sol in Scorpio, Luna in Aries.

Rising to a great height. It is raining red fire, and I surge upward through the fire. It rolls off me as I move upward without difficulty.

Upward, ever onward, ahh, through a moonlit landscape and then through a sunlit land, and finally I arrive in a volcanic realm, with molten lava visible all around me. A red-winged bloody angel appears in the sky. I test him, and he passes.

He says: Zonzna-mad is my name.

These letters appear in dripping blood, from right to left from my point of view, on his forehead. He points with a fiery wand to an erupting volcano in the distance. Orange-red lava pours out everywhere.

I am on a mountaintop overlooking this valley. It is nighttime, yet the valley is eerily lit by the stars and the glow of the erupting volcanoes. He says:

I am the angel of Fire.
Behold not the trembling earth,
for within its volcanic depths lieth the salamanders.

---

23 Capricorn, Caput Draconis, Sagittarius. Geburah in Yetzirah. Governors' names appear on the Tablet of Earth.

The creeping stuff of life,
never extinguished by the waters of Love.
The Fires, cooled by the Waters,
forming the rock of all life on earth.
Thus Love washes over Will,
solidifying Forms for future development.
Like the flowing lava takes on new form
when it hits the sea, extending the reach of land.
Thus do Love and Will interact
to create the root Forms of all that is to come.

A blazing golden calvary cross appears in the sky, with a dark stone, like onyx, at its center. Figures (as on a Grecian urn) revolve around me in the blackness as I am drawn into the stone. They appear as the band of the zodiac, or as scenes of battle.

Arrows are fired, and a goat appears. The great head of a dragon overarches the whole scene. Zonzna-mad's voice booms out:

The Dragon and the Arrow and the Goat are One,[24]
For the execution of Will flyeth forth as an Arrow,
With the great fiery breath of the Dragon,
Flying through scenes of folly,
Of seeming death and destruction,
Yet ringing out with the laughter of eternity,[25]
The laughter that ringeth forth
When Love under Will is accomplished.

Zonzna-mad bids me exit. I fall down a shaft, toward my body, and find I have returned.

---

[24] Caput Draconis, Sagittarius, and Capricorn, respectively.

[25] The previous two lines refer to the mysteries of the Devil Atu of the Tarot and thus Capricorn.

ɜ˥ɫ

THE CRY OF THE 24TH AETHYR, WHICH IS CALLED NIA[26]

Friday, October 26, 2007. Approximately 5:30pm. Sol in Scorpio, Luna in Taurus.

Rising high, like a vast and endless upward tunnel.

Above the clouds the sun and the sky, above the sun, space and blackness. A turbulent sea, a volcanic realm above this. I pass further up. I perceive the space as a cauldron of cloud, and a moon in is the sky. Pan appears. Or perhaps a centaur of some kind. He bears a staff in his right hand, it has a skull. I test him and he fails.

I strive to rise upward but am blocked. This is the realm of NIA. The air moves like water. The air is viscous and slightly obscures vision. Filtering all I see. There are many cubes, each on a circular pedestal. The cubes are blue—the blue of Chesed in the Queen scale. There is a mist hovering at about the level of the cubes, sometimes rising toward their tops, never obscuring them.

The clouds part above, and a bearded angel with a lightning flash appears. The sky is lit by the lightning flash—all is illuminated. I hear the voice, and speak it:

Sonf, sa bia a s noan amizpi.[27]
Sonf, sa bia a s noan amizpi.

---

[26]Scorpio, Sagittarius, Taurus. Chesed in Yetzirah. Governors' names appear on the Tablet of Earth.

[27] Roughly: "Reign, and the Voice of Four will be fastened." A Mystery of the Grade of Adeptus Exemptus. The concepts of rulership, the quaternity, the lightning flash, the cube, the appearance of the angel, and the color blue all seem to refer to the powers and nature of Chesed/Jupiter, the ruler of Sagittarius.

Sonf, sa bia a s noan amizpi.

The Enochian letter Ↄ appears before me, at the level of the great angel, who appears almost as a god, crowned and with flowing beard.

A trumpet blast resounds—the angel himself appears to play it. All dissolves into liquid silver light, running like paint in the sky and on the surface of the ground below.

I am one with this painted light. I dissolve into a pool, the pool swirls, and I have returned.

THE CRY OF THE 23RD AETHYR, WHICH IS CALLED TOR[28]

Monday, October 29, 2007. 10:45pm. Sol in Scorpio, Luna in Cancer.

I rise high. The field of stars opens to me—the sky is as the bowl of a great Graal.

A dragon of stars appears, the fire from his mouth the only visible shape other than the outline of his star-body. The moon, in first quarter, is visible in the sky. I am somehow in deep space yet also the moon is here. The stars are Her veil.

A great, brilliant whiteness breaks forth, and the veil is rent. Blinding whiteness.

I am enraptured with the sense of a great Presence. A being with a body of flaming light, I am embraced by this being of light! It is my own Angel. I know His touch.

This is the light beyond the dark. The eternal light. [Several minutes pass in silence.] Stillness. There is only light, and there is nothingness.

A ZAX[29] moooah ip.
Orocha vovim, Mad ipam.

---

[28] Caput Draconis, Libra, Pisces. Binah in Yetzirah. Governors' names appear on the Tablet of Earth.

[29] The name of the 10th Aethyr

Loholo la zod zimii IAIDA.[30]

Continuously, crowns are placed on my head. This is the Yetziratic impression of the influx of the light into the crown chakra. Yes, the CROWN chakra! The image of the halo is like one frame in a motion video of this column of light, continuously pouring from above. A single frame would show one ringlet of stars like a classical halo, but the reality is of a never-ending influx.

And now I feel the light descending, sweeping down over my physical body. It is transforming my body. Every cell...sweeping down across my torso, legs, and feet.

Wave after wave, increasing speed. So beautiful. A beautiful blessing of stars.

Blessings and thanks to thee O Σ, O guardians of TOR, and to the Highest Light that I serve. Make me a vessel of thy Light, that I may serve thee, and manifest that Light in the world, by his Holy Name, Σ.

It is finished.

---

30 Roughly:

In ZAX repent not.
Underneath the Dragon, God is Not.
Shining first, they enter God, the Highest.

THE CRY OF THE 22ND AETHYR, WHICH IS CALLED LIN[31]

Tuesday, November 6, 2007. 7:30pm. Sol in Scorpio, Luna in Libra.

I rise high. I am frustrated—the process is a struggle tonight. I feel a dryness. Finally, after a few minutes:

I move through layers of landscapes, ending on a moonlit plain with dark silhouetted mountains in the distance. A unicorn appears—a phantom—dismissed with a banishing pentagram.

I rise higher still, and will to see the rose color keyed to this Aethyr. This immediately bursts forth, and I behold circle of whirling (counter-clockwise) stars in the heavens, like the zodiac belt but horizontal and directly above.

This becomes a giant column of light. All is fragmented, all is One and many. Whirling in every color as the iridescent cloak of Raziel.[32]

I see these Atu: Chariot, Art, and Death.[33] I am shown the mystery of charging the chariot into the Cup of All, the Graal. The blending of the Fire and Water, charging into Death and the Bliss of Death.

The brief vision concludes, and I have returned.

---

[31] Cancer, Sagittarius, Scorpio. Chokmah in Yetzirah. Governors' names appear on the Tablets of Air, Water, and Earth.

[32] The archangel of Chokmah

[33] The Atu corresponding to the letters in the name of the Aethyr

THE CRY OF THE 21ST AETHYR, WHICH IS CALLED ASP[34]

Wednesday, November 7, 2007. Approximately 11pm. Sol in Scorpio, Luna in Libra.

I rise to a great height, to behold 10 concentric spheres. They are made of the sea, but somehow not of water. They are composed of some sort of plasma, of life-force itself.

It is daylight, and a full sun is in the orange-hued sky.

This changes to a field of pure white—like snowflakes of light. I am surrounded by this gentle storm of light.[35]

A flaming Chariot appears, then lovers embracing – the Hierophant overseeing the ceremony.

I am admitted into Kether. The Hierophant is bearded and crowned. I am instructed to meditate on the canopy of stars that now circle about my head. The moving channel of light streams into my Crown center once again, as in the vision of TOR – an overwhelming influx of light! The Hierophant's hands are upon my head!

A voice cries out:

Saga toltorn zomd ip.
A micalp sonf luciftias –

---

[34] Taurus, Virgo, Leo. Kether in Yetzirah. Governors' names appear on the Tablet of Air.

[35] It appears that the Seer was rising from Tiphareth to Kether at this point in the vision.

Luciftias zong nza.
A Mad, par pire a Ripir.[36]

A choir of angels sings. It is like the sound of doves. The notes themselves are as wings all around me. The notes and the Crown are One. The notes and the Hands of the Hierophant are One.

We are in the Chariot together, blazing a white road through the dark-space cosmos. Faster we fly, and now into a white sphere we are absorbed.

I ask for further instruction in the wisdom of ASP, and a great tower of Light appears. The instruction IS the tower, an infinite obelisk of light.

The All Father, the Infinite One. The Mystery is taught.

The Point of the Obelisk, infinitely small, is an infinite taper to that one dimensionless point. The mysteries of the Infinite One are the mysteries of the infinitely small—the infinitesimal Point of view. The Source and Goal of all Existence.[37]

The Vision is ended, and I find I have returned.

[Note: A scrying of the 20th Aethyr, KHR, was performed around this time (mid-November 2007) but the voice-recorded results were lost before transcribing. The Seer repeated the scrying of KHR (out of sequence) in October 2008, and the results follow.]

---

36 Roughly:

One creature in the midst of Not.
The mighty ruler of Light--
The Light of Wind and Motion.
In God, they are Holy, with no Place.

37 This paragraph describes the perception of Kether by the Yetziratic mind.

THE CRY OF THE 20TH AETHYR, WHICH IS CALLED KHR[38]

Tuesday, October 28, 2008. 10:45pm. Sol in Scorpio, Luna in Scorpio.

After rising high, quickly, I find myself in a mauve expanse—the sky is mauve, with silhouetted mountains in the distance—a clear resemblance to the two hills on the Moon Atu.

Anubis approaches, bearing a staff in his right hand. A curious intertwined double crescent moon appears in the sky. Ah yes, I see that it is the sigil of Pisces.

Anubis gestures toward the sigil with his staff, and bids me to fly up to it. I fly up, backing into it. I find myself in the sky, arms outstretched as in sign of Osiris Slain.

I am a source of lunar light. I do not see the sun, yet I know that I reflect forth its light to the landscape below.

I chant the Aethyr's name once more, and everything in sight turns bright red. Fires on the horizon—a great circle of fire. I float above the earth, and I behold the fire at the horizon all around.

Hoor-paar-kraat appears as on the Aeon Atu, with Ra-Hoor-Khuit at his center. There is a great trumpet blast, and I see that the flames themselves are the souls of all humanity. The infinite flux and reflux of souls, passing through the threshold that has been

---

38 Fire, Air, Pisces. Malkuth in Briah. Governors' names appear on the Tablet of Air.

called death, into the infinite invisible beyond. And somehow recycling, eternally.

This is the path of the Fool as well – the Step, in any direction. Aimless, yet Perfect. All manifestation, constantly cycling, regenerating.

The gates of the unconscious mind admit the fire and the air.

The dark and shadow are but ghostly images to fool the weak and the fearful.

And I have returned.

ΩLΩ

THE CRY OF THE 19TH AETHYR, WHICH IS CALLED POP[39]

Tuesday, November 27, 2007. Approximately 10pm. Sol in Sagittarius, Luna in Cancer.

I behold a great sea, and a whirlwind has brought me here. A spinning vortex, and yet there is a calm sea under a moonlit sky.

I see chariots flanking the scales. This is a place of Balance. It is the sea of consciousness, collective mind.

Islands begin to arise – points of individual consciousness. Now some begin to drop back down into the water as others rise. A continuous and eternal cycle.

A horn blows and two great flaming charioteers cross the sky, one from each side. Flaming, they charge toward the moon, which drops into the water. All is black.

The end times of consciousness — the end of Mind.

Then a glow comes from the sea. A golden sphinx arises from the water, vast and self-luminous, bearing a sword. I understand that I am to take this sword. I do so, and elevate it to the heavens, and a new moon appears in the sky.

The Scales balance on my upraised sword.

I ask for instruction from the Governors of POP.

---

[39] Cancer, Libra, Cancer. Yesod in Briah. Governors' names appear on the Tablet of Air.

A crowd of masters, bearded and robed, appears in a semicircle before me. The robes are of brown silk, except One in the center wearing crimson and silver. He is hooded, and the hood has silver trim.

He pulls back the cowl of his hood and I see a progression of visages:

First the head of a lion,
And now that of an eagle,
And now that of a man,
And now that of a bull.

He pulls his cowl forward again.

This is the lesson of Balance. As with the sword, as with the scales, as with the sphinx. Balanced Mind, Balanced Power, Balanced Kerubs.

And a final teaching from my Lord. He says:

I am Σ, the Destroyer of Falsehoods![40]

I give thanks to the Lords of POP and I return.

---

40 This vision presented multiple solutions to the falsehoods of Thought. Firstly, overcoming the delusion of the individual mind as a separate entity; secondly, the Right Relationship to subconsciousness; and finally, the balancing of mind via the symbols of the Sphinx. See the kerubic symbolism of the Universe Atu and the Path of Tav, which leads from Malkuth to Yesod, the sephira to which this Aethyr is attributed.

[Enochian script]

THE CRY OF THE 18TH AETHYR, WHICH IS CALLED ZEN[41]

Wednesday, November 28, 2007. Approximately 9pm. Sol in Sagittarius, Luna in Leo.

I rise high. A bright yellow orb surrounds me. An aged hermit approaches, this time in white, with a brown outer robe, and a staff in his right hand.

He gives his name as OZAZMA.[42] I test him and he passes, so I ask for instruction.

I am shown a Grail, hanging beneath a great blazing star in the sky. The star is Kokab,[43] and the Grail is the mind. The mind as a receptacle for the stardrops of light.

I ask for more guidance. The scene changes to great open sea at dusk. The Grail and star remain, but the starlight is orange, and in the west as at dusk.

A great Serpent appears in the water, as in the Scorpio Kerub.

A voice cries:

---

41 Leo, Virgo, Scorpio. Hod in Briah. Governors' names appear on the Tablet of Air.

42 The language was not specified within the vision. [Enochian script]=65, and means literally "make me" or "make us". Taken in Hebrew, עזאזמא=126.

43 Often attributed to Hod/Mercury, with its doctrines pertaining to the role of the human mind in relation to the macrocosm.

Lust for Death! Then is the true Hermit revealed![44]
Lust for Death! Then is the true Hermit revealed!

I fall into the water – this is my death, and I embrace it, then I emerge.

I am of the water, and One with the water.[45]

I am made of the sundrops of light that have fallen in the Grail. Indeed, I have been swimming in the Grail.[46]

Each drop of sunlight, a hermit-like yellow, one among many, None embracing All.

APO PANTOS KAKODAIMONOS!

And I have returned. It is finished.

---

44 The key words here appear to correspond to Leo/Lust, Scorpio/Death, and Virgo/Hermit. The doctrine implied pertains to the revelation of the Hidden Light within, once the illusion of individual existence has been destroyed.

45 This is the macrocosmic Water—the Great Sea itself—rather than the mere intellectual "water" attributed to Hod.

46 The concept of "fiery water" is a mystery of Hod, and of practical magick.

THE CRY OF THE 17TH AETHYR, WHICH IS CALLED TAN[47]

Friday, November 30, 2007. 11:45pm. Sol in Sagittarius, Luna in Virgo.

I have risen to crimson field of color. The atmosphere is in motion, as wisps of cloud only fleetingly visible.

I see the Priestess enthroned, but now she changes into the Hierophant, and then all are dissolved by the sweep of the scythe of the skeleton of Death.[48]

All seems silent and still, but then the vision is rent, and I behold a starry night sky.

The sky is filled with blood, and I know that the blood is an offering. The blood is soaked into the stars like a sponge absorbs liquid. An offering made and accepted.

A voice booms: Before thou may pass on, thou must tell me my name!

In response, I call out the name of the Aethyr.

The whole vision seems to be composed of points of light and color, like a pointillist painting. It fluctuates in color as if each point of light were another entire universe – a glimpse into a moment in some other world, visible for an instant before flipping to the next.

---

47 Caput Draconis, Taurus, Scorpio. Netzach in Briah. Governors' names appear on the Tablet of Air.

48 Caput Draconis, Taurus, Scorpio, respectively.

I step into this multifarious vision. My Body of Light has become the screen on which these visions appear. The stuff of my Body is one with these visions.

And then all is gone but the field of stars. There is no more instruction here, and I return.

THE CRY OF THE 16TH AETHYR, WHICH IS CALLED LEA[49]

Sunday, December 9, 2007. Approximately 11pm. Sol in Sagittarius, Luna in Sagittarius.

I rise high, mindful of the number of concentric circles through which I passed.

I hear the sound of angelic singing, high and piercing, yet brilliant and lovely. A soft blue sphere surrounds me. The earth shudders. All is pixilated once again, and coming apart. I am afloat in the soft blue.

I see the Chariot, and the aged Hermit with the lantern. He lights the way for the Chariot's path. The Hierophant is in the Chariot, or behind the Chariot on the path.

I behold three paths of light in the sky. They appear like the aurora borealis in texture, but as three golden rays of light pouring from beyond into the pale blue. I understand this to be the supernal influence upon Tiphareth.[50]

A great king appears, opens a book, and points to a picture. This becomes a vortex into which I am drawn. It is bluish white—a tunnel—with pulses of light on the outside. I am moving rapidly but not uncomfortably, and I pass through.

I am as a babe. I am as a babe. I am as a babe.

---

49 Cancer, Virgo, Taurus. Tiphareth in Briah. Governors' names appear on the Tablet of Air.

50 That is, the Paths of Zayin, Heh and Gimel, connecting Tiphareth with Binah, Chokmah, and Kether, respectively.

All is light and wonder. New knowledge. I am as a babe, and I remain in the bliss.

I have returned to my body but I remain very still and peaceful. I feel the embrace of Σ as he held me in his arms on our wedding day, in this very spot.[51] In the Sign of the Pyramid[52] I call for thy instruction, O my Lord Σ.

He says:

All is peace, my child.
Be not afraid.
I embrace thee in thy going.
I embrace thee in thy longing.
I embrace thee in thy sorrow.
I embrace thee in thy hating.
I embrace thee in all things my child.
Thou art my chosen, my infinite, my most lovely.
In the seat of thy soul do I dwell.
From thine eyes do I behold all splendor.

His words are ended for the time. All is peace, and I enter the Sleep of Siloam. A sleep unlike any I have felt since that fateful day when I lay within the circle and first fully embraced my Lover.

I say to Him:

And Thy Instruction, my Beloved, began with a whispering.
And thy caresses came forth in all of life.

---

51 The climax of the Seer's attainment of Knowledge and Conversation had taken place in the same spot in the Temple a number of years prior to this vision. This is a notable aspect of this particular vision, as the 16th Aethyr corresponds to Tiphareth in Briah – the place of the breakthrough of Briatic consciousness into Yetziratic mind, signifying (and actually *defining*) the attainment of full Knowledge and Conversation.

52 A personal Sign/posture communicated to the Seer by his HGA years before. It is used to call for Instruction from the Angel.

I have longed for an ever more penetrating touch.
To ride as the Charioteer on the flaming path of thy Will!

Ah yes! Send me forth, for I am thine,
My lord and lover and God.
Guide my path. Guide my mind.
My every thought, word and deed.
Guide my pen, my mind, my heart,
That I may ever serve thee
And manifest thy glory unto All!

TON! TON! TON![53]

It is completed.

---

53 In Enochian, "All! All! All!" These words were spontaneously spoken by the Seer with no knowledge of their meaning, but their import is clear in the context of the previous passage.

LΓL

THE CRY OF THE 15TH AETHYR, WHICH IS CALLED OXO[54]

Thursday, October 30, 2008. 11:40pm. Sol in Scorpio, Luna in Sagittarius.

I rise high, counting the circles.

I see great scales in the sky. The balance of all things.

The Stasis of earth, kept in balance by the eternal play of opposites. The Universe itself, embodying stability through balance.

I call for a guide, and a warrior on horseback appears, bearing a lance. He is dismissed with pentagram — a phantasm.

A great golden bearded countenance appears in the sky. His eyes are of fire, without any visible pupils. His face looms in between the scales. I test him and he passes.

I ask for a name, and he answers ZAZTADI. Give me thy number!, I say, and he answers 39.[55]

Communicate to me the mysteries of OXO, O Zaztadi!

---

54 Libra, Earth, Libra. Geburah in Briah. Governors' names appear on the Tablet of Air.

55 If the name is rendered זאזטאדי, this is a correct answer. 39 is the number of יהוה אחד, "Tetragrammaton is One" (or similar meanings). 39 is also 3 x 13, and thus expresses the Trinity as a Unity. This is a foreshadowing of the Sacred Triad, which is revealed in the vision of the 2nd Aethyr.

I behold a lone tree, on barren and windy hillock. Leaves catch the sunlight in the breeze. This is the Tree of Eternal Change.

The grass is vibrantly green. The brisk wind keeps changing directions, but the tree stands motionless. The sky is dark but somehow the sun is bright.

Figures move like wraiths upon this plain, earthbound. These are human souls in incarnation. Ones who cannot see the Tree, or its wonder.

This image fades, and I am back in the presence of Zaztadj.

The sky becomes red — the red of Geburah. A great rift opens up in the sky—I fly upward into it.

There is nothing but blackness beyond the red. Ahh! I see nothing but the body of Nuit. I plunge into her folds, into her folds! O Continuous One! O Density of the Stars, so great!

The serpent power! My spine convulses…I am crowned…I am crowned! I behold the Throne of the Adeptus Major.

I speak His Name, ∑, again and again. I will refine this energy, in His Name.[56]

I give thanks to Z for his guidance. I leave the field of olive. I have returned to my body. License to Depart and Closing.

---

56 This last sentence is essentially a very condensed Oath of Geburah and Adeptus Major. Having attained conscious knowledge of True Will with K&C, the Adeptus Minor strives to enact that Will in the world. Fulfillment of this Right Action is one marker of the attainment of Adeptus Major.

THE CRY OF THE 14TH AETHYR, WHICH IS CALLED UTA[57]

Monday, November 3, 2008. 11.30pm. Sol in Scorpio, Luna in Capricorn.

I rise to a great height.

I float amidst a swirling amber vortex. I am at the center of the vortex, and above it.

I see the letters of the name of the Aethyr, and there is a whirling fire.

There is disarray visible from certain vantage points: confusion, fear. I see it as the pure dynamic force behind all surface appearances of evil.

The truth. The veil of nature.

The hand of the Hierophant draws me up through the center of the flame.

Through the veil and into the flame I fly.

---

57 Capricorn, Caput Draconis, Sagittarius. This Aethyr is alternatively called UTI. Chesed in Briah. Governors' names appear on the Tablet of Fire.

Right spiritual governance rests solely in the ability of the Hierophant, that is, the spiritual leader, to draw near to the flame, to embody the Source, as the One Focus for those who Follow.[58]

I am at rest, with focus on the single flame at the Crown chakra.

The brief vision fades and I return.

---

58 A doctrine of Chesed. The spiritual leader (an Adeptus Exemptus, in the present context) is not the Source itself, but she must be a Focus of that hidden light from beyond the Abyss, in Thought, Word, and Deed, so that those in the outer world have a visible beacon to follow.

THE CRY OF THE 13TH AETHYR, WHICH IS CALLED ZIM[59]

Monday, December 15, 2008. Approximately 11pm. Sol in Sagittarius, Luna in Leo.

Rising to a great height.

I behold a magnificent river of fire. It is a river and yet also a lion or similar beast simultaneously.

I am afloat on this river of fire, moving quickly. I see the human figure of the Art Atu, appearing huge in the sky above me.

Ahh. We seem to be going towards the stream, the merged stream, as on the card. Yet the flow is toward the card rather than away from it.

There is a crown of nine stars about the head of the figure. These are arranged in a slightly elongated semicircle.

I somehow know that they are of the Nine, and I am of the Ten. I seek a guide to explain this mystery further.

A book is lowered from the sky, its pages turning as if blown by a great wind. I see a glowing red Teth in the book, taking up most of the right-hand page.

The pages flutter. The book closes and reopens.

---

[59] Leo, Sagittarius, Aquarius. Binah in Briah. Governors' names appear on the Tablet of Fire.

Now Samekh appears in blue.
Now Heh in blue-green.

I am instructed that the nine stars are these three letters in all their manifold expressions — as they are expressed in each of the Gunas, for this is a threefold mystery of Binah.

I understand that this book was previously lost, and that these mysteries involve my initiation beyond the fourfold and fivefold mysteries of the Serpent-Cross[60] — my entry into threefold Supernal mysteries.

I grow weary, and the vision seems to be fading.

I give blessings and thanks unto the lords of ZIM. Be there peace between us until I return.

And I have returned to my body.

---

60 These were specific mysteries and formulæ revealed to the Seer during his climactic K & C working.

CL7

THE CRY OF THE 12TH AETHYR, WHICH IS CALLED LOE[61]

Tuesday, December 16, 2008. 11:30pm. Sol in Sagittarius, Luna in Leo.

I rise high.

I find myself struggling upward past a field of blue water — no, it is grass.

I arrive. A sphinx sits before me on a desert plain. Now I see that there are multitudes of sphinxes, stretching out as far as I can see.

A cloudless blue sky is above, now changing to night sky, yet somehow the sphinxes are brightly lit. The sand is golden.

Myriad rows of black-robed figures with white turbans are visible on the plain before me, endlessly interspersed amongst the sphinxes.

One approaches. He is bearded, with dark skin. I give the pentagram and he vanishes. Another appears — I test him and he passes.

---

[61] Cancer, Libra, Virgo. Chokmah in Briah. Governors' names appear on the Tablet of Fire.

I ask his name, and he answers: ZASKIMRAN. I ask his number, and he answers 147.[62]

What mysteries of LOE will you show me?

A pale-skinned, golden-haired infant is brought forth from the bowels of one of the sphinxes. It is is oddly motionless, almost like a figurine.

Zaskimran smashes the infant over his knee, and it breaks into pieces. Clearly it is made of stone or ceramic.

"Kill thyself!" a disembodied voice commands.

I see a diamond on the ground, released by the breaking of this figurine. It is huge, perhaps inch in width, and perfectly cut. Zaskimran picks it up and hands it to me, and I clasp it in my hands.

Now I am in the diamond. I perceive shining through it, reflected in all the facets, a pure light. This grows all around me — I am surrounded by mirror-like reflections of pure light. It seems to come from beyond… as if I am looking out through an outer wall of the diamond, from within.

A voice cries:

Resolve these images into one, and thou shalt know the Crown!
Be thou the charioteer.
The diamond is in the Graal!
Retrieve the diamond and become the Light.

---

62 The language was not specified in the vision. The number 147 has no clear connection to the name Zaskimran, when taken either in Hebrew (389) or Enochian (543).

The balance of the diamond, the one seed, the one light.[63]
Force and fire, and the Graal.
Here is truth.

The instruction is ended. I dismiss Zaskimran, with blessing and thanks.

A dove descends from above and drops a yellow-gold ring, which I grasp and place on my left ring finger. A crown of similar yellow-gold is placed on my head, also dropped by the dove.

A voice cries: Thou hast known the Crown. Let it be ever thus.[64]

Blessings and thanks to all who abide in LOE, I say. Peace be unto you.

And I have returned to my body.

---

[63] This is another reference to the four- and five-fold mysteries discussed in the previous vision—a four-sided diamond, with its Light as the Fifth Element. The "Seed" mentioned here is a foreshadowing of the Word discussed in the vision of the 2nd Aethyr which, along with the present vision, also corresponds to Chokmah.

[64] This was a command to maintain the state of consciousness induced by the events of the vision.

ᒣᒷᗺᕮ

THE CRY OF THE 11TH AETHYR, WHICH IS CALLED IKH[65]

Sunday, September 13, 2009. 1pm. Sol in Virgo, Luna in Cancer.

I rise to a great height, counting the Aethyrs as concentric circles as I fly upward.

There are storm clouds, and beyond them a churning light. Dark mountains are visible on the horizon.

The sky splits from the center as if rending a veil, and I behold the three letters of the Aethyr's name.

Flaming steeds appear, pulling a chariot. The charioteer is garbed as a Roman, with a plumed helmet. He rides past without a word.

An eagle appears, with some sort of branch, flowers or twigs in its mouth. The eagle is white, with a suggestion of gold. It grows into a towering, flaming angel, bearing a book. The angel says:

See thou the fire of love! (and He indicates the flames which curl around Him)
Hear thou the Voice of the fire of love:
Shall not the eagle and the sparrow lie down?
Shall not the mountains be torn asunder?

Aye, the time is near, for the fires of love toil evermore.
Ever under the surface of All.
Seek not the highest for thou art there.
Seek not the lowest for thou art there.

---

65 Sagittarius, Fire, Air. Kether in Briah. Governors' names appear on the Tablets of Water and Fire.

In these abide.
In these plunder.
In these toil.
In these tear asunder.

The middle way is thine,
but not until the heights and depths have been traversed.

I am the angel of Kether,[66] guardian of IKH.
Speak no more of this name,
for it is I that speaketh in this place.
Where I am there is no cloud and no fire,
Though I am of fire and of cloud.
Where I am, I am.[67]

אהיה[68] is the key to the pinpoint of Light beyond All.
Though it is the master key.
There are many gates to this place.
All who seek, all who know, all who strive, all who Go, find me.

The Angel dissipates into golden sparks which rip apart the entire scene, as a great sun, golden-red in the heavens, becomes the only thing in sight.

I ask for a guide, and the Sun intensifies. This is the Star.

My vision is divided. The lower field with the blazing radiance of the Sun, and the upper field absolute blackness. An Absence even of consciousness. An utter Void. How absolute!

---

66 The appearance of the Angel suggested he was actually the archangel Metatron, but he did not name himself as such. It may be that his injunction to "speak no more" of the name of the Aethyr also referred to an unconscious reflex in the mind of the Seer to name him as Metatron.

67 See *Exodus* 13:21 for context on the "fire" and "cloud" mentioned here. Also, "I am" is a key-phrase of Kether.

68 A Divine Name of Kether. (See previous note.)

This is the boundary between non-existence and existence. Each enveloping the other, as in the Tao. Each implying the other. Each existing by virtue of the other.

I enter the Void place. Blackness. Now sparks.

A curtain of light streaming from what appears to be "above".

Faster! I am in a cylinder of golden light. A single beam of light, expanded.

The Sun is at my Crown. Now I am in the Sun! Ah!
The cylinder rotates clockwise. The energy moves. A voice:

Send forth thy pegasus into the world!
That path of air, thou knowest!
Thy folly is beautiful!
Thy fear is nought!
Thy step is perfection!
Thy path is eternal![69]

The vision fades. Blessings unto the Lords and guardians of this place, which shall not be named again this day! Blessings and thanks unto thee by the light of my holy Angel, whose Name is known to me! Blessings and thanks!

I return to my body.

---

69 These passages appear to involve the Path of Aleph (The Fool), which joins Kether to Chokmah.

THE CRY OF THE 10TH AETHYR, WHICH IS CALLED ZAX[70]

Saturday, September 19, 2009. 10.10 pm. Sol in Virgo, Luna in Libra.

I rise high—with a feeling of strain as I break through the membrane into the 10th Aethyr.

The sky is bright yellow, flecked with black.[71] The light is as flame. These sparklings of light are the atmosphere itself.

I call for a guide. A great hulking beast of stone appears, but dissipates when a banishing pentagram is given.

I call again for a guide. The earth greens, plants spring forth. They are the guide. They are one consciousness moving together as green growing things upon the earth's surface.

They grow into an arched doorway/trellis of a sort. Their greenness shades the bright sun overhead. I begin to walk through.

A double-door parts at the center and a great light breaks through at the end of the corridor. I pass through this door, which is of old wood, into a field of nothing but sunlight. Not a field in the earthly sense but a field of Light.

---

70 Leo, Taurus, Earth. Malkuth in Atziluth. Governors' names appear on the black cross, with the addition of an L.

71 Yellow is the King Scale color of Malkuth, while yellow, rayed black, is the Princess Scale color. This fusion of Atziluthic and Assiatic colors, in combination with the appearance of Metatron (the archangel of Kether) later in the vision, suggests the doctrine, "Kether is in Malkuth." See also the previous vision, where Metatron seems to appear, but is not named.

My guide here is a bearded angel, the Sun appearing to blaze from the center of his chest. He says:

I am Metatron come forth to Malkuth.
My staff is of light.
My eyes are of light.
Thou hast chosen the way of light, child.
Enter in. Believe in my Kingdom, which is thine.

He motions beyond himself, further in the direction I have been traveling. I still see nothing but light, as if the sun is nearby and blinding everything with its light, but the sun itself is not visible.

Now I see the sun fully eclipsed on a field of stars. And now I see the band of the Milky Way with this blackened sun in the foreground. It is as if I am in space, looking at the sun and into the galaxy beyond.

A golden flaming Aleph appears upon the black sun itself, and begins to whirl clockwise, throwing off sparks. It has become the whirling svastika. The sun itself begins to rotate clockwise as well.

I say: I am I., prophet of Σ the Holy One, come forth to ZAX for the furtherance of the Great Work. What further lessons hast thou for me, O Lords of ZAX?

I see horizontal lines, as if lines of text moving past too fast to read and comprehend. Every book of the Universe is being written before me.

Every book, every thought. The mind of the Universe itself conveyed in the language of time and space. The Great Mind Manifest in time and space. The mystery of Malkuth of Atziluth.

Blessings and thanks to the Lords of ZAX.

I return to my body.

THE CRY OF THE 9TH AETHYR, WHICH IS CALLED ZIP[72]

Monday, November 9, 2009. 12:45pm. Sol in Scorpio, Luna in Leo.

After rising to a great height, I call to the Lords of ZIP:

Show forth thy mysteries! I am I,[73] prophet of ∑.

I call for a guide, and a flaming lion-crab appears. A spectre—banished with a pentagram.

I push higher and repeat the Governors' names. I hear a voice inwardly:

The lust of the Art bears thy Self forth to dissolve in the Grail.

A great Grail appears in the night sky, starlit. There is light from an obscure source, glowing across mountain peaks.

A point of light appears from the center of the domed sky-ceiling much like the oculus at the Pantheon. This grows brighter, coming down upon me as a cone. I am taken up in the light, toward the oculus.

I now see that I am looking out through the oculus, and the round dome is the surface of an eye, looking outward. My body is in the

---

[72] Leo, Sagittarius, Cancer. Yesod in Atziluth. Governors' names appear on the Tablet of Fire.

[73] I is the first letter of one of the Seer's magical mottos.

shape of a pentagram, filling the oculus as I look out into space and time.

I know that I am the eye of God. A voice cries:

See thou the Grail of the Stars. The All!
Perfect thyself, as the pentagram,
and thou shalt fit rightly in my pupil.

Now flames appear, as if the eye is moving, or a corridor of flaming light is streaming toward me. I am still in the eye, gazing outward.

And now the corridor of flame is within the eye itself, and the eye is traveling. This is travel through time.

The flame of the Art, the Lust of the Art. Ah! The oculus and light is the grail chapel, as in Parsifal. I was drawn up into its source—Atziluth. The center of the ceiling of the Vault.

Yes! Yes! The Grail awakens the eld of the All-Father.[74] The transmission of the Light from Beyond, filling the Grail with its ever-flowing and ever-abundant lifeblood. We feed this lifeblood and partake of it and return it, eternally.

The eye of God looks down as Light. Creative light issuing forth from vision. I create as I see. And as I see, it is created.

The Eye of God is expressive. Vision begets existence. The sight of God creates, as an expression of the Thought. The Word is Light. For the Word is created patterns, seen by the vision of the Eye of God.

---

74 The All-Father resides in Chokmah (Wisdom). Thus is this Grail of Binah the "shrine of the winds of Wisdom" referenced in the vision of the 27th Aethyr.

This is instantaneous. All perception, thought, manifests its own patterns, to the extent of the strength of the perceiver. Perception is creation, in every day, in every moment. We are the eye of god, creating our world through our vision of the world.

A voice:

Form the patterns as thy Will.
There is no law beyond Do what thou wilt.
These patterns will manifest, by virtue of your perception!
Seek to perceive that perfection of Will which is thine own.
Then will the patterns that thou perceivest
Match those on the trestleboard of the highest.

Swallow up these patterns as seeds.
These desired and desirable ones.
What will grow?
Thou knowest. Thou knowest. Thou knowest.[75]
From beyond the beginning to beyond the eternal end.
Thou knowest.

I give blessings and thanks unto the Lords of ZIP, and find I have returned.

---

75 The references to "seeds" and triadic forms are foreshadowing the doctrines of the Sacred Triad revealed in later visions.

THE CRY OF THE 8TH AETHYR, WHICH IS CALLED ZID[76]

[N.B. This particular vision was obtained using a specially constructed ritual format which incorporated eroto-comatose lucidity techniques. See Part Two of this book for the full ritual procedures.]

Wednesday, December 2, 2009. Approximately 9pm. Sol in Sagittarius, Luna in Gemini.

I see a sharp mountain peak set against a violet sky with a crescent moon. The whole scene is in shadow.

My vision clears. There is light, and the mountain peak is revealed to be a fire triangle.

It is now bright daylight, yet somehow the stars are visible. I am in the desert, and the fire triangle has formed into a pyramid. Two jackals stand before it, and a whirl of cloud is above its apex, rotating clockwise. The cloud descends as a pillar to meet apex of triangle, and the capstone of the pyramid disappears as the light reaches it.
Now I am in the center of the pyramid, which I can now see is four-sided. The light from the cloud above pours down upon me. This is the union of lingam (pyramid) and yoni (circular white cloud.)

---

[76] Leo, Sagittarius, Spirit. Hod of Atziluth. Governors' names appear on the Tablet of Fire.

There is Fire inside the pyramid, and I stand burning within it! My soul is enraptured in the fire! Golden arrows fire upward from my being into the cloud above.

Lords of ZID, bring the vision of thy realm to my consciousness! Instruct me in thy mysteries! They answer:

Flame forth as the pyramid in all thy going, O Phallus of Light![77]
In thy fire thou shalt burn up thyself.
The winds shall carry thee forth as an offering of Love
To the altar of Air.
The altar of Air shall be upraised in the column of Fire.
Upraised as the milk of the stars.

The light of each star grows more and more intense. They seem like pinpoints at first, then they grow and appear like millions of winged angels of light. Then they grow further still until it seems the entire space between the stars is filled with light. I am inside a globe of light. All that is, is this globe. This Oneness, giving birth to all Forms.

Within this globe of light, I am now traveling at the speed of light. All around me is empty blackness, but I bring the light. The traces of the light create worlds as I pass, forming galactic patterns across the universe.

Now I am back in the Pyramid, and I am still burning. Four holy altars are visible on each side of the pyramid, but I know them to be inside of me. Circular table of violet velvet sits directly under the oculus, with a crystal sphere at its center.
Before me, on the first altar, are flowers of pink and violet.
On the altar to my right, a dagger with a hilt of black and gold.
On the altar behind me, a golden plate.
And on the altar to my left, swirling incense smoke.

---

[77] Πυραμισ=831=φαλλοσ

These are the elements of the Pyramid of Life.

Now I am out on the plain—the desert is silver. There are many pyramids, each a life, an incarnation.

I behold the entire Universe, in the pupil of an Eye. Each Universe creates the next. The Gaze of one Eye manifests the next, which then gazes upon another. Each point of consciousness embodies its own divine Mind, and possesses its own creative Vision.

There is a man in a blue robe, seated on a camel.[78] I follow him through a bronze archway and into a courtyard overlaid with gold.

A fountain of black water is there, and a cup of black and gold. I fill the cup with water from the fountain and I drink: Golden light bursts forth from my Crown.

Transparency of the Self is the key to Right Perception of life, and all the Universe. The more transparent we are as the Light shines through us, the clearer our vision of the universe this Light reveals. When our Self is fully transparent—invisible—a perfect prism for the light—we see things as they are.[79]

I return again to the pyramid, but now the capstone is golden and aflame. The circle of Cloud still hovers above, extending as a column downward to touch the pyramid.

---

78 Blue is the King Scale color of the path of Gimel, which means "camel."

79 Here the Seer is confronting mysteries of the annihilation of the Individuality; not merely Ego-disidentification for the sake of aspiration to the Angel/ Superconsciousness. Now, all selfhood is dissolved and made transparent. The entirety of the human life a mere outline through which the One Light is channeled.

And a golden Ankh manifests in the midst, as the Union of the Pyramid and the Circle.

And with this the vision is ended.

THE CRY OF THE 7TH AETHYR, WHICH IS CALLED DEO[80]

Sunday, November 28, 2010. Approximately 6pm. Sol in Sagittarius, Luna in Virgo.

I rise high, counting the Aethyrs along the way. The vision comes easily.

I behold a blood-red sky. I am in the center of a circle of gold. At first it appears to be mountains, but now I see I am sitting on a sphere, within this blood red atmosphere. I am floating, presumably with empty space beyond.

I am as large as the whole planet itself. The gold circle is actually the horizon all around me.

Hawks and vultures appear. I draw a banishing pentagram and these disintegrate — phantasms.

Send forth a guide, O Lords of DEO, for I am set forth to scry thy Aethyr. I am the servant of the same god as you, a true worshipper of the highest! I am the prophet of the Serpent-Cross, and its Light. I am come to seek thy mysteries. Send forth a guide for I., servant of ∑ the Holy One.

There is Silence, as if a clearing of mist. Then a winged steed appears, an aged hermit riding upon it. He gives his name as

---

80 Spirit, Virgo, Libra. Netzach in Atziluth. Governors' names appear on the Tablet of Fire.

SIMKA.[81] I test him with "Do what thou wilt…" He responds with "Love is the law…" and refers to me as "My Lord ∑". This strikes me as odd, but those are his words.

I ask for instruction. He replies: Hold not back one drop!

A golden pyramid with a shining white capstone appears in a starlit sky. Behind the capstone is a solar disk blazing, yet the night sky is mostly dark. Many other stars are visible.

SIMKA points at the capstone. I move up to the capstone and see a small gap between it and the pyramid. The individual stones of the pyramid are visible.

Many men, appearing tiny from my vantage point, are shaping the stones of the lower section with chisels. This is perpetual work, never-ending. The pyramid is always being built. The capstone is untouched, eternal, not made with hands. The capstone is itself a smaller pyramid, and its form defines the shape of the full pyramid in each completed lifetime. Each incarnation adds its own lower pyramid to the capstone, but the finished form is merely a reflection of that which the capstone has embodied from the beginning of time.

I transcend this vision, rising above a layer of cloud. The sun is now visible. SIMKA on his winged steed flies beside me as we move across and above the layer of cloud. His skin is golden, his beard and hair white. His noble face is set with deep indigo eyes, as deeply colored as the night sky, with multitudes of visible stars. He bears a crook in his right hand and a scimitar in his left. These are his weapons.

We travel onward to a green valley. Golden scales are balanced at the tip of another pyramid. The capstone is the fulcrum point.

---

81 סימכא=131

The lower part of the pyramid must be built in right balance, and the determination of that balance depends on the apprehension of the nature of the capstone — its placement and size in perfect harmony with what is below. That is, the pyramid must be constructed so that every facet of its construction honors the position and nature of the capstone.

Much as the King's head must be placed perfectly beneath the Crown for the Crown to descend[82], so must the pyramid be builded rightly for the capstone to descend and be fitted. The Universal Life Crowns the Individual Life when the Individual Life assumes the proper form and place.

I move back up into the sky with SIMKA. Clouds begin to whirl, alternating clockwise and counter-clockwise; rhythmically, at a pace which reminds me of fast breathing.

The breath of the universe.
Winding and unwinding.
Systole and diastole.
I am not afraid to die.

Death shall be the Crown of All.
Death shall be the Crown of All.
Death shall be the Crown of All.

I shall mingle my life with the universal life.
Confundum animam meam cum animam universum.

May my life be an offering of the perfectly builded pyramid,
That the capstone may find its rightful place.
And may the silent seed of self within me,

---

82 That is, the Right Positioning of the Adept (as Tiphareth, the King) for the descent of the Angel's Light (from Kether, the Crown.)

Expressed in my individual life,
Return in full remembrance of its Source.

That Source which is truly the seed bearing within itself
All needed forms, and embodying the simple form which is the
Extension is the individual life —
Which, in infinite extension, is the arc of all lives
As the soul develops, in its own ecstasy.

As a crystal grows, as a fractal expands, so does the seed
Reach ever outward and upward eternally, in replication;
A ripple in universal time and space,
In the ecstasy of its self-perpetuation.

So goes each individual life.
Life after life after life.
Repetitions of the seed pattern, to the glory of that Star-Self,
In its unfolding majesty and ecstasy.

Thanks unto SIMKA and the Lords of DEO for thy vision and thy wisdom. May I remain in remembrance of this vision, for the performance of my own Great Work, which is the Will of my Lord Σ.

I return to my body, and remain in holy meditation for a time.

Interpretive Note

The particular dimensions of a capstone are sufficient to define the shape of the pyramid below--it is in this sense "holographic". Just so, the Seed of Self resident in Neshamah defines the "shape" of the personality which developes to serve it. The Adeptus Exemptus, having brought the Ruach (the pyramid, in this particular metaphor) to its full potential, must then discover the "capstone" or Seed which explains and defines all that he has been in mortal life. In some senses, this Seed represents the expansion of the True Will concept into the realm of the infinite—that is, the universal motive behind the particularized expression of Will that has been lived out at the level of the individual incarnation.

The Adeptus Exemptus is a perfected human, in the usual sense. He has attained a pinnacle in his field; he is well-known due to his excellence and his "published" works (whether strictly so or not.) Yet he is not able to completely revolutionize the world in which he lives, for he has not yet fully and consciously become a vessel of Universal Will. Once he pours himself into the Cup of Babalon, and is willing to give up all he has in Service of the One Will, he attains to Binah. Then, and only then, can he lead others by his own light (outwardly); for inwardly he is simply shining forth with the light of Universal Will that he has only now become able to wield.

As Adeptus Exemptus he was limited by his vision of self and its relation to the universe. His light was dimmer, and could only "attract" (energetically) those within a certain subset of his field—a school of thought, such as a theoretical orientation within psychotherapy or physics. The Magister Templi, on the other hand, will be the voice of a completely new vision, a complete paradigm shift in human consciousness of some type. Yet there is more growth to come. The Magister Templi must then discover the seed principle (deeper still than the "capstone seed" sought by the A.E.) by which he was impregnated. What was the Word which, when planted in the soil of Binah, grew into the garden tended by the Magister?

The Magus has identified with that original motive principle, and has the Wisdom to see its inevitability—the necessity of its being. His presence in the world is the seed of growth and change —of evolution itself. That is, his mere presence simply *changes things,* entirely in accord with the universal Will which he IS, consciously and (behaviorally speaking) *reliably.*

Ɛ✗Ꝑ

THE CRY OF THE 6TH AETHYR, WHICH IS CALLED MAZ[83]

Monday, December 20, 2010. Approximately 10:45pm. Full moon, near winter solstice, total lunar eclipse. Sol in Sagittarius, Luna in Gemini.

Rising through Aethyrs, counting them as I pass.

I am inside a sapphire. In gold I see the name Ɛ✗Ꝑ. I move outside the sapphire, and find that I am in a field of golden grass. A full, huge moon in a blue sky above. It is mid-day, and the sun is bright.

I see that the sapphire is some sort of vessel for my own travel in these realms. It is perhaps to be used henceforth. It has brought me here.

I look around and the golden grass stretches far in all directions. The landscape begins to spin, and I re-enter the Sapphire. I call out: Lords of MAZ, send forth thy vision, pleasing to my eyes and discernible to my mind, that I may bring forth the fruits of thy wisdom into my life in all the worlds, that the hierarchy of light may be fulfilled through the agency of my life, for I am I., prophet of ∑, servant of the Serpent-Cross, and its Light.

A booming voice cries:

Servant of the Serpent-Cross, welcome!

---

[83] Aquarius, Taurus, Leo. Tiphareth in Atziluth. Governors' names appear on the Tablet of Fire.

The world of MAZ is open to thee, for thou hast perished!
Thou hast perished indeed!
Thine eyes have grown dark.
Thy mouth has become mute.
Thy brain has been exposed to the searing rays of the sun,
and has burnt to a fine dust.

Thy life has been mingled with the universal life!
Thou hast known No-Thing.
Thou hast cast away the dark.
Thou hast embraced the dark.

Thou hast eaten of the dung.
Thou hast transmuted it to gold.
Thou hast made gold with gold.
Thou hast given away thy gold.

Thou hast prostrated thyself before the feet of the altars of Gheber.
Thou hast inverted thyself under the wings of thine Angel.
Yes, we knowest, we knowest, O I.
Thou hast journeyed far.
Thou hast come hither through the four worlds.
Thou hast loved, and hated, and played amidst the waters,
slept amongst the trees; the air bore thee in its bosom.
Thou hast been wholly burned in the fire.
I., thou art welcome! Thy new name is....S.[84]

Lords of MAZ, I seek more visions! Share of thy wisdom with I., whom thou hast admitted and welcomed to thy realm. I am the servant of ∑ the Holy One! I seek to serve All. Let my life be a token of this truth of my Will.

---

84 The motto of He who dwells in the City of the Pyramids, first revealed to the Seer in this vision.

A lion appears in a starlit sky. I seem not to have moved, but the sky has changed to an incredibly dense array of stars. The lion is simply staring at me. He looks to his left, my right, where a brilliant star grows brighter and brighter in the sky.

I am taken into this star, and wholly subsumed by its brilliance. It is like a tunnel, but there is no motion, only brilliance. A flame of light with no heat. Now, like individual flames of light, like each possibility is a flame in itself, but there is only one flame.

Now I am this flame—this singularity. I see the flame extinguished, and there is Night.

I see the pyramids, and Adepts filing past them and toward me, in two columns. They are gray, bearded, solemn. Some are bearing lights.

The stars above are now dark above this bleak scene. I turn to watch the procession of Adepts go off into the distance. They are going out to serve all life — many hundreds of them. They have been changed here. They are spectral here, like ghosts, but where they go they will be solid.

I chant the Aethyr's name many times.

I am inside the sapphire again. It is the most brilliant blue. I cry:

Lords of MAZ, I seek further wisdom of thy realm.
I am I.! I must proceed! I must go! I must die!
Help me to die, Lords of MAZ, that I may serve all life!
That in death, I may serve all life!
I fear not death! I fear not death!
Take of me what thou wilt,
for I have offered all of myself into the Grail of Our Lady.

Golden wings of light caress my head, as if they are hands laid upon me in consecration. My head is split. A golden seed of light is dropped directly into my Crown. This light fills my head, as if it is inside my head but also emitting beams of light directly upward, uniting with the Crown center.

I am to sit in contemplation, in silence. I know that the vision is complete. It was as if I was being "reprogrammed" by this light at the Crown. I was simply required to sit receptively and let the light work upon me.

Blessings and thanks unto the Lords of MAZ, for I am I., prophet of ∑, servant of the Serpent-Cross, and its Light. Many thanks for thy wisdom. Let thy gates be open unto me, that I may return at my Will. Until that time, farewell. May the light and the blessing of the Most High be upon thee. For I am a servant of the same God as you, a true worshipper of the Highest.

I return in the sapphire, downward. The egg of sapphire is solid and bright, and in it I find a smoother, safer, quicker passage through the Aethyrs. This is its use at this time.

And I have returned to my body.

THE CRY OF THE 5TH AETHYR, WHICH IS CALLED LIT[85]

First Vision[86]

Sunday, December 26, 2010. Approximately 11pm. Sol in Capricorn, Luna in Virgo.

High rising, counting the Aethyrs as I go.

Silver, the key—nothing but silver, I am in a sphere of silver, transformed from sapphire. The letters of the Aethyr appear in Enochian. And now in Hebrew: Cheth, Samekh, Gimel.

I cry:

Lords of LIT, I am I.! Bring forth thy vision!
I., Servant of ∑, approaches thy Portal.
For by the Chariot, and the Arrow,
and the Moon do I approach thee!
For I have given of my life into the Universal Life.
I have fired the Arrow of Aspiration!
I have bathed in the moonlight of our Lady!

I repeat the Governors names many times, with ever-increasing intensity. Ecstasy!

---

85 Cancer, Sagittarius, Caput Draconis. Geburah in Atziluth. Governors' names appear on the Tablet of Water.

86 As a reminder, to aid comprehension of what follows: "I" is the first letter of one of the Seer's mottos, ∑ represents the Name of the Seer's HGA, and "S" is the first letter of the Name of the Magister.

The silver sphere is now aloft in the starlit heaven. The Great Whore appears in the sky, riding the Beast. A scourge in her right hand. She has eyes of fire. Flailed am I! Flailed on my shoulders by her scourge!

She says:

Serve me only! Thou hast come from the dead land,
With a dead soul, and dead eyes.
Thou hast no right but to die in my love!
Give me All! Give me All! Give me All!

Thou shall be dust as I crush thy Universe.
Thou who was I., who art now S.
For this is thy name in this place, thou Nameless One.
The Arrow that shot thee forth
From the Foundation unto the Sun, flames no more,
For darkness surrounds thee and death is abiding with thee.
Refuse it not! Refuse it not, O Dead One!
For the ecstasy of All awaits.

Thou hast three tasks:

Defeat the Stone of thy birth!
Revel in its destruction!
Eat of the Lizard of Time!

When thou hast completed these in heart, then shalt thou be prepared for further initiation.

This is the lesson of LIT.
No more is needed.
Go forth from this place and return...as ye Will.

I descend in the silver sphere. And I am returned to my body, to lie in contemplation.

Second Vision

Sunday, January 2, 2011. 11.40pm. Sol in Capricorn, Luna in Capricorn.

I feel I have completed the 3 tasks "in heart" as Babalon said, and begun the extension of this into all levels of consciousness and behavior. I feel I am ready to approach LIT once more.

Rising to a great height, counting the Aethyrs aloud this time.

Flames are all around. Babalon is embracing me! Shudders up my spine and throughout my body. I cry:

Ah, Babalon!
Lady of Flame, Lady of Night,
Lady who ridest the Beast of seven heads!
Bring me thy vision, for I am I., Prophet of ∑ the Holy One!
I seek to Know in order to Serve!
I offer my service that I may be a perfect vessel
of the Universal Light.

She gestures behind, and a curtain parts revealing the night sky.

There is a crescent moon, and a beam of light from above creating a disk of light on the ground before me. She bids me enter, and I am taken up into the beam of light.

Birds of Fire! All around! I am through the clouds, above the Sun, in Space!

I am on the path of Cheth. I ascend to the Grail, and drink of it, for it is offered to me.

I climb into the great Grail, and I am awash in the Blood!
A high voice, gentle, somewhat distant, says:

I am S.! I am S.! I am S.!
I speak with the mouth of timelessness.
Divide the trees of eternity.
Seek not thy resolution in these things.
Divide the trees of eternity.
Seek thy resolution in the tapestry of time!

The Healer. The Killer. The Mother of All.
She awaits throughout…the Serpent…
The Serpents trails about the Sun.
The Serpent eats….and the Sun is dark.
S. speaks from without the Grail.
For within the Grail is None.
S. speaks. For without the Grail is None.
See the Land! See the land destroyed!

(I see fields of grain, burnt away by space into nothingness.)

The Voice continues:

S. speaks to I., the Little One:
I am S. thy Mother.
Thou wast placed here to Heal and to See.
The Grey Land is yours to Heal and to See.
The Serpent-Cross, Thy Father.
S. thy Mother.
Thou Art the Prophet I.!

The Serpent-Cross is in Chokmah.

S. is in Binah.
The Shin-Teth, the Fire of the All-Father,
Of Chokmah, flames forth.
That Seed of Fire is placed in the Grail of S.
What is thy Word, Serpent-Cross?
It is yet to be revealed.[87]
I, S., when united with the Serpent-Cross,
Shall reveal Thy Word, O Little One, I..

I ask for the mysteries of S. Let me be a vessel for the Words borne by the Grail of S. Let every moment be a parting of the Veil.

The Voice:

Mindfulness of this brings forth ecstasy.
The veil rent asunder.
The veil between the solid body
And the ecstasy beneath and beyond.

In the circle of fire, we have met again.

Yes, those are my words, little I.: "Under stars, the waterway glistens. We will meet here again, under stars, in this circle of fire."[88]

And the Vision is concluded.

Blessings and thanks to the Lords of LIT.

---

[87] See the vision of the 2nd Aethyr.

[88] These words originally occurred to the conscious mind of the Seer several years before this vision, and were used as song lyrics in the piece titled, "In Space, There Might Be North." In the present passage, S. is identifying himself as the Source of those words.

I, I., forth-speaker of S., Servant of ∑ the Holy One, Prophet of the Serpent-Cross, and its Light. We will meet here again, under stars, in this circle of fire!

I am to sit in contemplation. I am returned to my body.

Ω♐Ⴒ

THE CRY OF THE 4TH AETHYR, WHICH IS CALLED PAZ[89]

Friday, January 7, 2011. Approximately 8pm. Sol in Capricorn, Luna in Pisces.

I stand before a great veiled Goddess, huge and translucent in the Sky above a fertile plain. She casts her veil outward across the whole plain and upon me, and its luminescent strands fall around my body.

I am enwombed, as in a cocoon, which now becomes opaque. I am digesting myself. I am become nothing but an oozing liquid inside this cocoon.

Now I begin to take form. I have eyes. Now hands, arms and legs. My heart beats. I breathe.

My eyes open, and I emerge from the cocoon, beholding a brilliant green all around me. I am inside the sphere in which I have traveled, now as emerald.

The sphere shatters and a shard of emerald shoots upward, seemingly into the dark of starlit space.

I am one with this sliver of emerald.

I travel upward, ever upward. I offer myself to the great Goddess, for all that I have lies shattered below.

---

89 Cancer, Taurus, Leo. Chesed in Atziluth. Governors' names appear on the Tablet of Water.

All that I am, cast into shards.

I am befitted as a shard of perfect emerald. I pierce a pearlescent sphere of light, and the new organism grows. The seed, planted and received, grows.

The sphere grows in brightness and in size. Now it has overtaken my vision in every direction. I feel there is no separation between me and this….we are one organism.

A pearlescent sphere of light, ever-growing in brilliance and size.

I call out to S. for counsel: S.! Speak fair words of wisdom unto I.!

A voice:

I am S. and I speak unto I. the little one.
Child of the Star and the Snake, thou art befitted as emerald,
But thy journey has just begun.

Thou must go to the gray land of thy heart.
Plant the seed of emerald within.
This garden shall be thine.
Give its fruits to all who pass.
Give its bounty to all who ask.

I who am No-Man, in the One Place of All Time,
Command thee, little one.
Let that seed be planted and
Let the garden be rich with many fields.
And this then is a key, O little one:
7 10 3 5 A P Z 1 9 8 4 2 3.

Take this in English.

The letters and numbers.[90]
The key to thy garden, O little one, I.
I ask the Magister S.[91] for more instruction, and He says:

It is not for thee to ask, but to receive.
The key to thy garden has been given.
Take this further key: 7 4 5 8 9[92]
This in English.
And in Greek: TOPOS[93] TOPOS TOPOS.

Go now, I. Thy vision is complete. Thou hast all thou needest. Come again when thy task is complete.

I give blessings and thanks to the Lords of PAZ, and I return to my body.

---

90 If the letters in this key are converted to numbers using the English Qabalah Simplex (A=1 through Z=26) it enumerates to 95, the value of V.V.V.V.V. in Latin Qabalah Simplex, as well as אבן גדלה, "the great Stone".

91 It became clear in this Vision that S. was a Master of the Temple.

92 In EQS, this further key enumerates to 33, which is the value of M.M.M. in Latin QS, as well as גל, "spring" or "fountain".

93 This enumerates to 720 in Greek Qabalah. (See NOUS and KAIROS in subsequent visions.)

ꝑꝉꝫ

THE CRY OF THE 3RD AETHYR, WHICH IS CALLED ZOM[94]

Monday, March 7, 2011. Approximately 9:30pm. Sol is Pisces, Luna in Aries.

I rise high, counting down the Aethyrs very quickly as I fly upward. I see a vortex of whirling violet and white light. The face of Babalon is above the opening of the vortex. Her hair is aflame. In her eyes is a fire of light, of terror and of love. I say:

I am I., but thou hast named me S., O my Lady. Bring forth the vision of ZOM!

Confundam animam meam cum animam universum.

It is though her hands are around my shoulders. I am kissed on the forehead by my Lady Babalon. She says:

Thou who hast become No-Man, and who art now known as S.
Thou who art with the place of the All.
The no-place that is in thy heart.
The grey land thou hast visited.
The emerald shard has been planted.
In love and in devotion thou hast worshipped at the altars of All.
The Stone has been destroyed!
Its destruction is a revelation of fire and of pain and of death!
Thou art sad to see this O I.,
And thou art enraptured to see this O S.

Vision availeth not!

---

94 Leo, Libra, Aquarius. Binah in Atziluth. Governors' names appear on the Tablet of Water.

Even sight availeth thee not in this place.
For see the thunderous clouds in the distance?
Nothing can stop the coming storm S., O prophet!
Nothing can stop the coming storm.
Thou must surrender—surrender all!

I ask: How may I better serve the highest light, O lady?

She answers:

Cut off thy right side.
Cut off thy left side.
Attain unto the line that is the division between these.
The line that hath no width and no depth.
The line that is eternal and has infinite length.
The line that began before the beginning
And shall endure past the end of all things.
The line that runneth down the middle
Of thy left and thy right, Which are None.
Seek me only! Surrender!

I see a whirling halo of light in the heavens. There are wars in the heavens. Great chariots of flame and of mist. But these are as mere symbols of the depth of this meaning. For this is a war within the unconscious of mankind itself.

The symbols themselves are at war. The mind of man is at war. Insanity in the depths of the collective mind!

I seek to bring order and peace, that all may be in its right place, and harmony may be restored into the mind of humanity. How may I serve?

She answers:

Thou shalt know, S. Thou shalt know, when the time is aright.
For thou hast Wisdom in these symbols.
It is thy Way. Thou hast been prepared.

Speak fair words to the people.
Speak fair words of peace and harmony.
Speak fair words in the language of the people.
Deny thyself utterly, for thou hast no right but to do thy Will.

I cry: I seek keys, O Lady, for the execution of this task. Empower me by thy vision!

She answers:

In the equilibration of the Serpent and the Water-Bearer,
There is peace. Leo and Aquarius.
Seek that balance of Mind and Fire.
Offer the flame into my Cup.

In the equilibration of the Teth and the Heh
Shalt thou find peace, And bring peace, and be peace.
Thou, who wast once known as C.P.P.[95],
Shall know the right action
In the equilibration of these symbols.
For the lion is freedom and rejoicing, force and fire.
And the Water-Bearer, receptivity, reflectiveness.
And in the equilibrium of these are all things
Dissolved into their right forms.

The Vision begins to fade, my mind called away, distracted. I bring myself back to the vision, and behold again the face of my Lady Babalon, who again embraces me about the shoulders and kisses me on the forehead, right shoulder and left shoulder. For Centrum in Trigono Centri[96] is the seal, mark and chrism of this work.

I am instructed to sit in receptive silence, after which I return to my body.

---

95 The Seer's Probationer motto, which implies the creation of peace through Right Action.

96 "The Point in the Center of the Triangle." See the vision of the 2nd Aethyr.

THE CRY OF THE 2ND AETHYR, WHICH IS CALLED ARN[97]

Tuesday, March 8, 2011. 12:16 am. Sol in Pisces, Luna in Aries.

Rising high, counting down the Aethyrs.

I behold a scarlet sphere all around me, and a volcanic landscape beyond it.

Dry, dry, dry.

The horizon glows red, while the sky above appears as a wide oculus—about half of the visible sky is darkened starlit, and the rest is a scarlet glow. The earth is dry, brown and powdery.

A moving sphere of light approaches. It grows, transforms into the shape of a wizened old man, in a robe of blue with golden stars and golden trim. He bears a staff in his right hand, and a sphere of white light in his left. His eyes are a piercing blue. He touches the staff to my forehead, and all goes black.

I say: What is thy name, O Wizard? I repeat this, and I give a banishing pentagram in testing. He vanishes…a phantasm.

I cry:

Lords of ARN, bring forth thy Vision!
TOPOS TOPOS TOPOS!
I S., call thee forth, Lords of ARN!

---

97 Taurus, Pisces, Scorpio. Chokmah in Atziluth. Governors' names appear on the Tablet of Water.

The oculus widens and all above is now starlit.

One star grows large and bright, with many angular points of light —directly over my head in the visible sky. Through this hosts of angels descend, spreading out across the sky. The entire canopy of heaven is spangled and starlit with these angels of light—their wings leaving trails of sparkling light.

They sing:

We send thee forth to the grey land, S.,
That thou may return here,
Reabsorbed into the Word, the Logos.
Reabsorbed into the Seed of thy being.
Thou hast no words but thy One Word.
For in this word KAIROS[98] shalt thou find thy Being.
In the triangle of matter, supernal and material,
Shalt thou find thy Place and thy Mind.
The enveloping womb of Form.

In Kairos are all things in potential.
In Kairos are all things in manifestation.
In Kairos are No Things that are Not.
For Holy Time envelops all, includes All,
Exceeds All, encloses All,
Potentiates All, manifests All.

In Kairos did the world begin.
In Kairos did the world proceed and develop.
In Kairos did humanity find itself,

---

98 *Kairos* is "sacred time", as opposed to the chronological time of *chronos*. Kairos is "sacred" in the sense that it is always in harmony with the will of the Universe. Thus, a magician performing an operation in right relation with Kairos will always choose the perfect moment of action—qualitative, rather than linear/ quantitative, "good timing". In some versions of the Greek Orthodox liturgy, the ritual begins when the Deacon says to the Priest, "It is the time for the Lord to Act." (*Kairos tou poiesai to Kyrio).* Similarly, a magician acting in harmony with his or her True Will is, by definition, acting in accord with the Will of Universe.

And in Kairos will the Eye be closed at the End of Days.
Thou must bring that balance, Teth to Heh, balanced in the Lamed.

But here the great Initiator...
The great Initiator of the Unconscious is the passage of Death.
In the haze of the Moon springs forth life and regeneration.
None can see these unless they be Wise in Kairos.
For whoso Knoweth Kairos,
For whoso is Crowned in Kairos, Wise in Kairos,
Whoso Understandeth Kairos, yea yea yea,
HE shall knoweth the mysteries of rebirth, regeneration and life,
Springing from the apparent death—
That tragedy, so-called, so misnamed by the minds of men.
Indeed, this tragedy so called and so named IS the Initiator,
And out of it, the Scorpion, and the Eagle, and the Serpent.

Kairos, Topos, Nous.[99]
Kairos, Topos, Nous.
Serpens Crucis.
Centrum in Trigono Centri.
The Serpent-Cross.
The Eye.
Centrum in Trigono Centri. Kairos-Topos-Nous.

---

99 In this context, Kairos is equivalent to the Supernal "Night of Pan", NOX, where all possibilities exist. Kairos (as NOX, νοχ), Topos, and Nous each enumerate to 720 (Greek), thus forming a three-in-one Sacred Triad. It is of interest to note that the initials of the phrase, *Kairos tou poiesai to Kyrio* also enumerate to 720.

Any Magical Act can be understood, analyzed, and constructed, and its outcome evaluated, using this formula alone. Kairos is Right Timing—the choice of the appropriate moment (or conditions) when an Act is divinely warranted and, therefore, certain to be efficacious; Nous is Right Thought or Right Intention—the Logos of the Act, which formulates both the intended effect and the method of action; Topos is Right Place—the correct choice of the object of the Act, the magical link, and the precise Form of the desired outcome. See also the vision of the 1st Aethyr, where this Sacred Triad is mapped to the Supernal sephiroth. 720 is also the value of the Greek "priest" (*hiereus*), "holy spirit", and "seed", among other words.

The two key numbers.
Explore this in the Light of the Eye.
These mysteries are revealed in the Light of the Eye.
Kairos itself is a key to these numbers.
Take the number of Kairos,
Divide separately by each of the two key numbers.[100]
Find the value of these results as two separate numbers,
And this is the final key to the Serpent-Cross.

Understand All in Kairos.
Be Wise in Kairos.
Crown All in Kairos.
Destroy All in Kairos.[101]

I sit in meditation, under the night sky of ARN, in Remembrance of God.

Blessings and thanks unto the Lords of ARN. I S., and He who is beyond S., and THAT which is beyond All and is nameless, give thanks to Thee for thy Vision.

I am returned to my body.

---

[100] This is a reference to the two key numbers revealed in the vision of the 4th Aethyr, 95 and 33.

[101] Taking the value of KAIROS as 1—the Unity of Sacred Time—and performing the divisions as instructed gives .01 and .03, perhaps another reference to the concept of Unity-in-Trinity (and thus the Sacred Triad) with the Serpent-Cross at the Center. These four lines are thus interpreted as corresponding to Binah (TOPOS), Chokmah (NOUS), Kether (KAIROS), and the Point at their Center (Serpent-Cross). See the vision of the 1st Aethyr for more on this.

THE CRY OF THE 1ST AETHYR, WHICH IS CALLED LIL[102]

Friday, March 11, 2011. Just after midnight. Sol in Pisces, Luna in Gemini.

Rising to a great height, counting down the Aethyrs.

I am in an Egg of Gold, in a field of white, like snow composed of stars.

A flaming golden arrow soars upwards, striking into a red, equal armed Cross in the center of the cosmos. The edges of the Cross are aflame, burning without disintegration or consumption. The arrow struck to the heart of All.

Now beams of red-scarlet with golden flaming edges extend outward, infinitely. Thus is the material universe bounded and created. Thus does life spring forth from the source of All.

Space is curved. These four rays curve, fluctuate and pulsate, between their positive and negative poles. Plus one, minus one.

I see Ra-Hoor-Khuit, vast among the stars—commanding the stars themselves. His voice speaks:

S.! Thou holy one of holy ones.
Thou broken one of broken ones.
Thou tiny speck. Thou blazing sun!
Thy Will shall be done, if thou doest the Will of All!
Subsume thy Little Self in the womb of the All-being.

---

[102] Cancer, Aquarius, Cancer. Kether in Atziluth. Governors' names appear on the Tablet of Water.

This then is a Key—the final mystery of the Aethyrs,
For thy knowledge and thy garden. AZPOQRZ.
Take this in English, Hebrew, Latin and Greek.[103]
Let this be the Crowning Truth.
The Truth that reveals and hides.
That truth beyond the Water and the Fire.
That Truth of the Union of these things.
For the Voice of Fire is terrible and thunderous.
The Voice of Water limpid and receptive,
Aching with the Ecstasy of that Union
So Desired and so Desirable.

But beyond all these as the Water extinguishes the Fire,
As the Fire evaporates the Water.
Beyond all these things,
The Naught and Nowhere, Naught and Never!
Thus is Kairos Kether, Nous Chokmah, Topos Binah.

Even as the Triad exists in Binah[104]
As the gateway to the palace of the Supernals, [105]
So are the Supernals themselves this Triad.
For Sacred Time is that Dimensionless Point of perfection,
Beyond any vulgar Time.
And Chokmah contains the Seed of Mind,
That Fire of Creative Mind itself,
And Binah is the Fertile Place, awaiting the Seed.

---

[103] In English Qabalah Simplex, AZPOQRZ=119. In Hebrew (as אזפוקרז), 401, את, "essence" (See "alpha and omega", "azoth", and cognate ideas.) In Latin Qabalah Simplex, 103, IANUA ARTIS ("door (entrance, approach) of the Art"), ROTA MUNDI ("wheel of the world"). In Greek, 274, *sabao,* a Gnostic name of God, etymologically related to the Hebrew *tzabaoth,* which can imply "hosts" or "armies", as well as "stars."

[104] It is notable that the initials KTN (in Greek) enumerate to 370, the value of *oikos*, "house", and *olos*, "perfect". These ideas reinforce the form-giving and womb-like attributes of Binah.

[105] Consider that *neshamah* is the name of the Qabalistic "part of the soul" attributed to Binah, but also to the whole of the Supernal triad.

In my own voice:

I have sat in meditation on this Triad.
The Serpent-Cross, in the Midst of the Eye.[106]

Then the Flaming red cross of equal arms is enfolded upon itself,
Becoming a single point of flame.
Then even this is extinguished, and all the universe, all the stars,
Are drawn into a single point, dense and dark.

Yet in this darkness, the womb of the unknown,
Lies the Seed of Wisdom.
All potential.
The Seed and Secret of All Things.

In this Blackness did I witness the creation of the world.
In this Blackness now filled with Light.
In this Light the embodiment of Night.
So sayeth the holy ones of all times,
That the Truth be spoken in sign and symbol.

Once again I am in the golden egg in the field of white, like snow composed of stars. The whiteness is the incredible density of all of their light—like a sheet of pure light. Unlike anything I have ever beheld.

And the Crown hovers above my head. And the All-Father, the All-Mother, and THAT which is beyond these, gently rest upon my head, as the Crown of All. And I accept this burden willingly, knowing that it is not "I", but rather…

THAT which is beyond all I am
Who hast no nature and no name,
Who art, when all but Thou are gone,
Thou, centre and secret of the Sun,

---

106 That is, the pupil of the Eye in the midst of the Triangle formed by Kairos, Topos, and Nous. (See cover image.)

Thou, hidden spring of all things known
And unknown, Thou aloof, alone,
Thou, the true fire within the reed
Brooding and breeding, source and seed
Of life, love, liberty, and light,
Thou beyond speech and beyond sight,
Thee I invoke, my faint fresh fire
Kindling as mine intents aspire.
Thee I invoke, abiding one,
Thee, centre and secret of the Sun,
And that most holy mystery
Of which the vehicle am I.
Appear, most awful and most mild,
As it is lawful, in thy child!

I am irradiated with golden-white light. Ah! (My physical body is wracked with convulsions of ecstasy.)

Σ's Name repeated—His Presence enveloping me. Utter ecstasy! I am taken into the heart of All. All Love. I am witnessing the primal swirlings! I am witnessing...I am Remembering!

Lords of LIL, blessings and thanks for the Vision of the Majesty of the Primal Swirlings. Blessings unto the name of Ra-Hoor-Khuit, who hath taken his seat in the East at the Equinox of the Gods. Hoor in his secret name and splendor is the Lord initiating.

I am S., and I DO go forth into the land of the living. May the Light of the Highest be manifest in my every thought, word and deed, for it is my Will to manifest the Serpent-Cross, in all its forms and in all the worlds.

May KAIROS be the seal, mark and chrism of ALL! So may it be! Such are the Words!

The 30 Aethyrs are thus sealed and sanctified. May the Lord Σ place his holy hands upon my head, baptizing me with his Wisdom and Understanding, and Crowning me with THAT which is beyond these!

Such are the Words! So may it be! The deed is done!

Tetelestai!

Part Two:

Notes on Working Methodology

RECOMMENDED SCRYING METHOD

In spite of the complexity of the Enochian system overall, and the substantial inner development that is required to make the most of it, the procedures for scrying the Aethyrs are actually quite simple. There is no need for a meticulously decorated temple, and the only specialized equipment that is really needed are the Enochian tablets themselves. (In fact, one could reasonably argue that the recitation of the Calls is the only true requirement.) For Aethyr scrying (and for all my work with the Enochian system) I use the "reformed" tablets of Raphael, dating from 1587, colored and sigilized as usual, with Enochian rather than English lettering.

The temple is set up with a standard double-cube altar, on which is set a lighted white taper candle, *The Book of the Law*, the Tablet of Union, and the elemental tablet(s) on which the names of the Governors of the Aethyr to be scryed are found. Since this may involve up to five tablets including the Tablet of Union, it may be convenient to place the tablets on small tables or stands near the altar.

For recording the visions, it works quite well to have a handheld dictation device or smartphone app at the ready. Otherwise, the traditional technique of employing a human scribe will suffice. As usual, it is strongly suggested that you complete your diary entry as soon as possible after completing the scrying, preferably before leaving the temple.

I recommend the following procedure:

1. Dress in the robe and regalia appropriate for your Grade or degree. Otherwise, a simple white or black Tau robe will suffice. Prepare yourself with relaxation and rhythmic breathing.

2. Perform the Lesser Banishing Ritual of the Pentagram or the Star Ruby.

3. Perform the Lesser Banishing Ritual of the Hexagram. (The Star Sapphire is not a suitable substitute, as it is an invocatory ritual, not a banishing.)

4. Optional but recommended: Perform the Star Sapphire, Middle Pillar, or similar ritual as a general invocation.

5. Sit before the altar and tablets, and meditate on them silently for 3-5 minutes.

6. Read or recite the **2nd Call** in Enochian, then read or recite the **Call of the Thirty Aethyrs** in Enochian, inserting the name of the chosen Aethyr, as appropriate. These calls may also be read in English if desired, but the Enochian versions are a minimum requirement. (In spite of some traditional advice to the contrary, I have found that the use of the 2nd Call in this place creates the right receptive state in the consciousness of the Seer, "priming" it for what follows.)

7. Vibrate the names of the Governors, repeating as is felt to be necessary at any point in the working.

8. Externalize the astral body, or prepare a shewstone or magick mirror. (See my own *Living Thelema* (Cap. 11), and Aleister Crowley's *Notes for an Astral Atlas* and *Magick in Theory and Practice* (Cap. XVIII) for general suggestions on scrying and astral projection techniques, many of which will likely be quite useful in scrying the Aethyrs.)

9. Seeing yourself at the center of thirty concentric spheres, each of which represents one Aethyr, rise straight up in the astral body, counting the Aethyrs as you pass. Stop when you have arrived at the desired Aethyr. If using a shewstone or magick mirror, simply gaze into the scrying surface and allow images to

present themselves. Choose whatever technique works best for you.

10. Use the name of the Aethyr in Enochian script, and the Yetziratic attributions of the Enochian letters (e.g. the corresponding elemental or zodiacal sigils and Tarot cards) as keys to the vision. It may be useful to repeated visualize these various keys from within the vision, or as a means of intensifying your aspiration to begin to behold the vision. As noted above, it may also be helpful to repeat the Governors' names.

11. Use all scrying techniques known to you, including the testing of entities and the information they give you, according to your right ingenium.

12. When you feel the vision is concluded, thank the Governors of the Aethyr and any guides who have assisted you, and will yourself to *gently* return to your physical body.

13. Record the results of your vision and close the temple. Formal banishings (LBRP or Star Ruby, and LBRH) will rarely be necessary, but may optionally be done if you feel there is an unusual or bothersome amount of residual energy remaining in the temple.

RITUAL OF SCRYING THE 8TH AETHYR, WHICH IS CALLED ZID

incorporating Eroto-Comatose Lucidity[107]

Adept: Robed according to Grade
Assistants: plain white or black robe

The Temple:

The altar at center-east, with candle, *Liber Legis*, cup of water, censer and incense, Fire Tablet (appropriate for ZID); (Alternately, Cup and Censer may be placed on stands beside the altar, Cup to north, Censer to south)

A large mattress is placed west of the altar. Tools of the erotic arts are placed nearby so as to be easily accessible by the Assistants. A blindfold is ready for use of the Adept. Absinthe, wine, and/or other appropriate intoxicants are nearby for easy accessibility.

An unobtrusive audio recording device is prepared, and placed near the place where the Adept will be reclining, in order to record the Vision spoken by the Adept.

Incense: Jerusalem (equal parts frankincense and myrrh) or Abramelin

Very soft music is playing in the background. The volume should be low enough to avoid interference with audio recording of the Vision.

Preliminaries:

---

107 This is an outline of the ritual actually used to obtain the vision of the 8th Aethyr. Since it was developed for the use of a male Adept, it would need to be adapted to conform to the anatomy, physiology, and arousal patterns of a female Adept.

The Adept and Assistants perform ritual bathing and personal banishings. The Adept and Assistants may indulge in light use of intoxicants at this point. They robe, and spend 5-10 minutes in the Temple space utilizing relaxation exercises.

Banishing:

Lesser Banishing Ritual of the Pentagram

Purification by Water and Consecration with Fire

General Invocation:

Any suitable invocation of Nuit, according to the right ingenium of the Adept.

Proclamation:

I am I., Prophet of Σ, and it is my Will to scry the 8th Aethyr of ZID. May the guardians of ZID instruct me in the truths of their realm, for the furtherance of the Great Work.

Specific Invocations:

The Assistants begin manual and/or oral sexual stimulation of the Adept, as he proceeds with the 2nd and 19th calls, reciting the Governors' Names, and rising to a great height.

The Adept disrobes, is blindfolded, and reclines on the mattress. From this point onward, no words are to be exchanged between the Adept or the Assistants, except further invocations pertaining to ZID and its Governors, or words designed specifically to sexually arouse the Adept. (The Assistants may communicate quietly to each other if desired, but they should attempt to do so out of earshot of the Adept, who must have his full attention directed to the Vision.)

The Assistants resume sexual stimulation of the Adept by any and all means—but all stimulation must be **purely sexual** in nature. This may include erotic touch, sexually explicit language, restraint, and flogging or other light to moderate pain techniques, in addition to manual, oral and vaginal contact.

The Assistants should provide intoxicants to the Adept as they deem appropriate, but not so much as to encourage fatigue in the Adept. The intent is to stimulate the Vision. All fatigue must be a result of sexual exertion.

Stimulation of the Adept must be continuous, although the intensity may vary considerably. The Assistants take turns as appropriate to allow continuous stimulation. If the Assistants must take a break at any point, they place the Adept's hand on his penis, which signals that he must begin continuous self-stimulation until the Assistants return.

The Vision, Phase One (approximately 20-30 minutes):

Stimulation is gentle and gradual. The Adept reports any preliminary Visions. The Aethyr Name, and Governors' Names, may be repeated at will by the Adept and/or the Assistants.

The Vision, Phase Two (approximately 1 hour):

Stimulation is intensified, with the goal of keeping the Adept close to the point of orgasm over most of this time period. Further Visions are recorded as appropriate. The Adept may say "Slower" or "Stop" in order to avoid orgasm, if necessary.

The Vision, Phase Three (first orgasm and immediate aftermath, approximately 10 minutes):

At the appointed time, the Assistants bring the Adept to full orgasm, intensifying the release as much as possible through chanting of the Aethyr Name, as a mantram or otherwise. The Adept may also participate in this. The Adept's mind must be entirely focused on the object of the operation throughout the orgasm and aftermath. The Elixir is immediately offered to the Adept for consumption. The Adept reports any Visions in the immediate post-orgasm period. Sexual stimulation should resume after 10 minutes at most.

The Vision, Phase Four (additional orgasms, twilight sleep, and The End, approximately 1-2 hours)

Full stimulation is resumed. There may or may not be additional orgasms. Visions are recorded as appropriate. When it is apparent that no further orgasms will occur, the Adept is allowed to fall asleep. As soon as sleep begins, the Assistants rouse the Adept using only sexual means. **As soon as the Adept awakens, stimulation must immediately cease.** This pattern is repeated, and Visions are recorded, until such time as the Adept falls asleep and cannot be roused by further stimulation. At such time, the Adept is left to rest, accompanied by the Assistants if they desire.

THE 2ND CALL[108]

Adgt upaah zong om faaip sald, viiu L? Sobam ialprg izazaz piadph; Cas-arma abramg ta talho paracleda, q ta lors-l-q turbs ooge baltoh. Givi chis lusd orri, od micalp chis bia ozongon; lap noan trof cors ta ge, oq manin Iaidon. Torzu, gohe L; zacar, ca, c noqod; zamran micalzo, od ozazm urelp; lap zir Ioiad.

English translation:

Can the wings of the winds understand your voices of wonder, O you the second of the First? Whom the burning flames have framed within the depth of my jaws; Whom I have prepared as cups for a wedding, or as the flowers in their beauty for the chamber of righteousness. Stronger are your feet than the barren stone, and mightier are your voices than the manifold winds; for you are become a building such as is not, but in the mind of the All-Powerful. Arise, says the First; move, therefore, unto his servants; show yourselves in power, and make me a strong seething [seer]; for I am of Him that lives forever.

108 For details on the Enochian language and its pronunciation, Donald Laycock's *The Complete Enochian Dictionary.* (Weiser/Red Wheel, 2001) is highly recommended.

THE CALL OF THE THIRTY AETHYRS

Madriax ds praf [Aethyr name], chis micaolz saanir caosgo, od fifis balzizras Iaida! Nonca gohulim: Micma adoian Mad, iaod bliorb, Soba ooaona chis luciftias peripsol; Ds abraasa noncf netaaib caosgi, od tilb adphaht damploz, tooat noncf g micalz oma, lrasd tofglo marb yarry IDOIGO; od torzulp iaodaf, gohol: caosga, tabaord saanir, od christeos yrpoil tiobl, busdir tilb noaln paid orsba od dodrmni zylna. Elzap tilb, parm gi peripsax, od ta qurlst booapis. L nibm, oucho symp, od christeos ag toltorn mirc q tiobl lel. Ton paombd, dilzmo aspian; od christeos ag l tortorn parach a symp. Cordziz, dodpal od fifalz l smnad; od fargt, bams omaoas. Conisbra od avavox, tonug. Orsca tbl, noasmi tabges levithmong; unchi omp tilb ors. Bagle? Moooah ol cordziz. L capimao ixomaxip, od ca cocasb gosaa; baglen pii tianta a babalond, od faorgt teloc vovim. Madriiax, torzu! Oadriax orocha, aboapri. Tabaori priaz ar tabas; adrpan cors ta dobix; yolcam priazi ar coazior, od quasb qting. Ripir paaoxt saga cor; uml od prdzar, cacrg aoiveae cormpt. Torzu, zacar, od zamran aspt sibsi butmona, ds surzas Tia baltan; odo cicle qaa, od ozazma plapli iadnamad.

English translation:

O you heavens which dwell in the [nth] Aire, which are mighty in the parts of the earth, and which execute the judgment of the Highest! To you it is said: Behold the face of your God, the beginning of comfort, Whose eyes are the brightness of heavens; Who provided you for the government of the earth, and her unspeakable variety, furnishing you with a power of understanding, to dispose all things according to the providence of Him that sits on the Holy Throne; and Who rose up in the beginning, saying: the earth, let her be governed by her parts, and let there be division in her, that the glory of her may be always drunken and vexed in itself. The course of her, let it run with the heavens, and as a handmaid let her serve them. One season, let it confound another; and let there be no creature upon or within her the same. All her members, let them differ in their qualities; and let there be no one creature equal with another. The reasonable creatures of the earth, let them vex and weed out one another; and the dwelling places, let them forget their names. The works of man and his pomp, let them be defaced. The buildings of her, let them become caves for the beasts of the field; confound the understanding of her with darkness. Why? I regret that I made man. One while let her be known, and another while a stranger; because she is the bed of a harlot, and the dwelling place of him-that-is-fallen. O you heavens, arise! The lower heavens underneath you, let them serve you. Govern those that govern; cast down such as fall; bring forth with those that increase, and destroy the rotten. No place let it remain in one number; add and diminish, until the stars be numbered. Arise, move, and appear before the covenant of his mouth, which He has sworn unto us is His justice; open the mysteries of your creation, and make us partakers of undefiled knowledge.

THE GOVERNORS OF THE AETHYRS[109]

	NAME OF AETHYR (and tablet(s) on which Governors' names appear)	NAMES OF GOVERNORS
1	LIL (Water)	OCCODON, PASCOMB, VALGARS
2	ARN (Water)	DONGNIS, PACASNA, DIALOIA
3	ZOM (Water)	SAMAPHA, VIROOLI, ANDISPI
4	PAZ (Water)	THOTANP, AXXIARG, POTHNIR
5	LIT (Water)	LAZDIXI, NOCAMAL, TIARPAX
6	MAZ (Fire)	SAXTOMP, VAVAAMP, ZIRZIRD
7	DEO (Fire)	OPMACAS, GENADOL, ASPIAON
8	ZID (Fire)	ZAMFRES, TODNAON, PRISTAC
9	ZIP (Fire)	ODDIORG, CRALPIR, DOANZIN
10	ZAX (drawn from the "Black Cross"; use all tablets)	LEXARPH, COMANAN, TABITOM
11	ICH	MOLPAND (Water), VSNARDA (Fire), PONODOL (Fire)
12	LOE (Fire)	TAPAMAL, GEDOONS, AMBRIOL
13	ZIM (Fire)	GECAOND, LAPARIN, DOCEPAX
14	VTA (Fire)	TEDOOND, VIVIPOS, VOANAMB
15	OXO (Air)	TAXAMDO, NOTIABI, TASTOZO
16	LEA (Air)	CUCNRPT, LAVACON, SOCHIAL

109 See Dee's *LIBER SCIENTIAE, AVXILII, ET VICTORIAE TERRESTRIS ("The Book of Knowledge, of Might, and of Terrestrial Victory")* for the original names of the Governors of each Aethyr. The names presented in this table have been corrected to conform with the tablets of Raphael.

	NAME OF AETHYR (and tablet(s) on which Governors' names appear)	**NAMES OF GOVERNORS**
17	TAN (Air)	SIGMORF, AYDROPT, TOCARZI
18	ZEN (Air)	NABAOMI, ZAFASAI, YALPAMB
19	POP (Air)	TORZOXI, ABRIOND, OMAGRAP
20	KHR (Air)	ZILDRON, PARZIBA, TOTOCAN
21	ASP (Air)	CHIRZPA, TOANTOM, VIXPALG
22	LIN	OSIDAIA (Air), PARAOAN (Water), CALZIRG (Earth)
23	TOR (Earth)	RONOOMB, ONIZIMP, ZAXANIN
24	NIA (Earth)	ORANCIR, CHASLPS, SOAGEEL
25	VTI (Earth)	MIRZIND, OBUAORS, RANGLAM
26	DES (Earth)	POPHAND, NIGRANA, LAZHIIM
27	ZAA (Earth)	SAZIAMI, MATHVLA, CRPANIB
28	BAG (Earth)	PABNIXP, POCISNI, OXLOPAR
29	RII (Earth)	VASTRIM, ODRAXTI, GMTZIAM
30	TEX (Water)	TAAOGBA, GEMNIMB, ADVORPT, DOXMAEL

ENOCHIAN ALPHABET

Enochian Letter	English	Yetziratic Attribution	Value
	A	Taurus	6
	B	Aries	90
	C, K	Fire	300
	D	Spirit (as ShT)	31
	E	Virgo	10
	F	Cauda Draconis	3
	G, J	Leo	9
	H	Air	1
	I, Y	Sagittarius	60
	L	Cancer (waning moon)	8
	M	Aquarius	5
	N	Scorpio	50
	O	Libra	30
	P	Cancer (waxing moon)	8
	Q	Water	40
	R	Pisces	100
	S	Gemini	7
	T	Caput Draconis	3
	U, V	Capricorn	70
	X	Earth	400
	Z	Leo	9

ABOUT THE AUTHOR

Dr. David Shoemaker is a clinical psychologist in private practice, specializing in Jungian and cognitive-behavioral psychotherapy. David is the Chancellor and Prolocutor of the Temple of the Silver Star. He is a long-standing member of O.T.O. and A∴A∴, and has many years of experience training initiates in these traditions.

He is the Master of 418 Lodge, O.T.O. in Sacramento, having succeeded Soror Meral (Phyllis Seckler), his friend and teacher. He also serves as the Most Wise Sovereign of Alpha Chapter, O.T.O., as a Sovereign Grand Inspector General and Bishop of Ecclesia Gnostica Catholica. David is the founding Past-President of the O.T.O. Psychology Guild, and a frequent speaker at national and regional conferences. He is also a member of the U.S. Grand Lodge Initiation Training and Planning committees, and he serves as an Advanced Initiator Trainer.

David was a co-editor of the journals *Neshamah* (Psychology Guild) and *Cheth* (418 Lodge). In addition to his essays in these publications, his writings have been published in the journals *Mezlim* and *Black Pearl*, and his chapter on Qabalistic Psychology was included in the Instructor's Manual of Fadiman and Frager's *Personality and Personal Growth*, an undergraduate psychology textbook. He was the compiler of the T.O.T.S.S. publication, *Jane Wolfe: The Cefalu Diaries 1920-1923*, and a co-editor of *Phyllis Seckler: The Thoth Tarot, Astrology, & Other Selected Writings,* and *The Kabbalah, Magick, and Thelema. Selected Writings Volume II,* as well as *Karl Germer: Selected Letters 1928-1962.* His popular *Living Thelema* instructional segments are presented regularly on the podcast of the same name, and the corresponding book was released in 2013.

In addition to his work in magick and psychology, David is a composer and musician. He lives in Sacramento, California.

www.livingthelema.com

Temple of the Silver Star - Academic Track

The Temple of the Silver Star is a non-profit religious and educational corporation, based on the principles of Thelema. It was founded in service to the A∴A∴, under warrant from Soror Meral (Phyllis Seckler), to provide preparatory training in magick, mysticism, Qabalah, Tarot, astrology, and much more. In its academic track, each student is assigned an individual teacher, who provides one-to-one instruction and group classes. Online classes and other distance-learning options are available.

The criteria for admission to the academic track of the Temple are explained on the application itself, which may be submitted online via the T.O.T.S.S. website. The Temple has campuses or study groups in Sacramento, Oakland, Los Angeles, Reno, Seattle, Denver, Boston, West Chester (Philadelphia-area), Toronto, Japan, Austria and the U.K. Public classes are offered regularly; schedules are available on our website.

Temple of the Silver Star - Initiatory Track

The Temple of the Silver Star's initiatory track offers ceremonial initiation, personalized instruction, and a complete system of training in the Thelemic Mysteries. Our degree system is based on the Qabalistic Tree of Life and the cipher formulæ of the Golden Dawn, of which we are a lineal descendant.

Our entire curriculum is constructed to be in conformity with the Law of Thelema, and our central aim is to guide each aspirant toward the realization of their purpose in life, or True Will. In order to empower our members to discover and carry out their True Will, we teach Qabalah,

Tarot, ceremonial magick, meditation, astrology, and much more. Our initiates meet privately for group ceremonial and healing work, classes, and other instruction. We occasionally offer public classes and rituals.

Active participation in a local Temple or Pronaos is the best way to maximize the benefits of our system. However, we do offer At-Large memberships for those living at some distance from one of our local bodies.

If you are interested in learning more about our work, we invite you to download an application from our website and submit it to your nearest local body, or to contact us with any questions.

totss.org

Do what thou wilt shall be the whole of the Law.

The A∴A∴ is the system of spiritual attainment established by Aleister Crowley and George Cecil Jones in the early 1900s, as a modern expression of the Inner School of wisdom that has existed for millennia. Its central aim is simply to lead each aspirant toward their own individual attainment, for the betterment of all humanity. The course of study includes a diversity of training methods, such as Qabalah, raja yoga, ceremonial magick, and many other traditions. A∴A∴ is not organized into outer social organizations, fraternities or schools; rather, it is based on the time-tested power of individual teacher-student relationships, under the guidance of the masters of the Inner School. All training and testing is done strictly in accordance with *Liber 185* and other foundational documents.

Those interested in pursuing admission into A∴A∴ are invited to initiate contact via the following addresses:

A∴A∴
PO Box 215483
Sacramento, CA 95821
onestarinsight.org

The Student phase of preparation for work in A∴A∴ begins by acquiring a specific set of reference texts, notifying A∴A∴ of the same, and studying the texts for at least three months. The Student may then request Examination. More information about this process is available via the Cancellarius at the addresses given above. Please use only these contact addresses when initiating correspondence.

If you are called to begin this journey, we earnestly invite you to contact us. Regardless of your choice in this matter, we wish you the best as you pursue your own Great Work. May you attain your True Will!

Love is the law, love under will.

Made in the USA
Middletown, DE
21 April 2024

53297702R00070